T0284993

JEFF SMITH: CONVERSATIONS

Conversations with Comic Artists
M. Thomas Inge, General Editor

Jeff Smith: Conversations

Edited by Frederick Luis Aldama

University Press of Mississippi / Jackson

The University Press of Mississippi is the scholarly publishing agency of
the Mississippi Institutions of Higher Learning: Alcorn State University,
Delta State University, Jackson State University, Mississippi State University,
Mississippi University for Women, Mississippi Valley State University,
University of Mississippi, and University of Southern Mississippi.

www.upress.state.ms.us

The University Press of Mississippi is a member of
the Association of University Presses.

Copyright © 2019 by University Press of Mississippi
All rights reserved

First printing 2019
∞

Library of Congress Control Number: 2019950206

ISBN 9781496824790 (hardcover)
ISBN 9781496824806 (paperback)
ISBN 9781496824813 (epub single)
ISBN 9781496824820 (epub institutional)
ISBN 9781496824837 (pdf single)
ISBN 9781496824783 (pdf institutional)

British Library Cataloging-in-Publication Data available

Works by Jeff Smith

PUBLISHED BY CARTOON BOOKS

The Complete Bone Adventures Volume 1 (b&w, sc) 1993
The Complete Bone Adventures Volume 2 (b&w, sc) 1994
The Complete Bone Adventures Volume 3 (b&w, sc) 1995
Bone Volume 1: Out From Boneville (b&w, sc and hc) 1995
Bone Volume 2: The Great Cow Race (b&w, sc and hc) 1996
Bone Volume 3: Eyes of the Storm (b&w, sc and hc) 1996
Bone Reader: The Making of the First Trilogy (b&w, sc) 1996
Bone Volume 4: The Dragonslayer (b&w, sc and hc) 1997
Bone Volume 5: Rock Jaw, Master of the Eastern Border (b&w, sc and hc) 1998
Bone Volume 6: Old Man's Cave (b&w, sc and hc) 1999
Stupid, Stupid Rat Tails (b&w, sc) 2000 (Drawn by Jeff Smith, Written by Tom Sniegoski);
     Riblet (Drawn by Stan Sakai, Written by Tom Sniegoski)
Bone Volume 7: Ghost Circles (b&w, sc and hc) 2001
Bone Volume 8: Treasure Hunters (b&w, sc and hc) 2002
Rose (color, sc and hc) 2002 (written by Jeff Smith, Illustrated by Charles Vess)
Bone Volume 9: Crown of Horns (b&w, sc and hc) 2004
Bone: The Complete Cartoon Epic in One Volume (b&w, sc) 2004
Bone: The Complete Cartoon Epic in One Volume (b&w, hc) 2004
Bone: 20th Anniversary Edition Box Set (color, hc, color by Steve Hamaker) 2011
Bone: 20th Anniversary Slipcase (color, hc, color by Steve Hamaker) 2011
Bone: CODA (b&w, sc) 2016
RASL Volume 1: The Drift (b&w, sc) 2008
RASL Volume 2: The Fire of St. George (b&w, sc) 2010
RASL: Pocket Book One (b&w, sc) 2010
RASL Volume 3: Romance at the Speed of Light (b&w, sc) 2011
RASL Volume 4: The Lost Journals of Nikola Tesla (b&w, sc) 2012
RASL (color, hc, color by Steve Hamaker) 2013
RASL Book One: The Drift (color, sc, color by Steve Hamaker) 2018
RASL Book Two: Romance at the Speed of Light (color, sc, color by Steve Hamaker) 2018
RASL Book Three: The Fire of St. George (color, sc, color by Steve Hamaker) 2018
Tuki: Save the Humans, 80-page Giant (b&w, sc) 2015

PUBLISHED BY SCHOLASTIC/GRAPHIX

Bone Volume 1: Out From Boneville (color, sc and hc, color by Steve Hamaker) 2005

Bone Volume 2: The Great Cow Race (color, sc and hc, color by Steve Hamaker) 2005

Bone Volume 3: Eyes of the Storm (color, sc and hc, color by Steve Hamaker) 2006

Bone Volume 4: The Dragonslayer (color, sc and hc, color by Steve Hamaker) 2006

Bone Volume 5: Rock Jaw, Master of the Eastern Border (color, sc and hc, color by Steve Hamaker) 2007

Bone Volume 6: Old Man's Cave (color, sc and hc, color by Steve Hamaker) 2007

Bone Volume 7: Ghost Circles (color, sc and hc, color by Steve Hamaker) 2008

Bone Volume 8: Treasure Hunters (color, sc and hc, color by Steve Hamaker) 2008

Bone Volume 9: Crown of Horns (color, sc and hc, color by Steve Hamaker) 2009

Rose (color, sc and hc) 2009

Bone: Tall Tales (color, sc and hc, color by Steve Hamaker) 2010

Bone Quest for the Spark Book 1 (color, sc and hc, color by Steve Hamaker) 2011

Bone Quest for the Spark Book 2 (color, sc and hc, color by Steve Hamaker) 2012

Bone Quest for the Spark Book 3 (color, sc and hc, color by Steve Hamaker) 2013

Bone Tribute Edition 10th Anniversary (color, sc and hc, color by Steve Hamaker) 2015

Smiley's Dream Book (color, hc, color by Tom Gaadt) 2018

PUBLISHED BY OTHERS

Shazam!: The Monster Society of Evil (written and drawn by Jeff Smith, Color, sc and hc). DC Comics, 2007

The Art of Bone (color, hc). Dark Horse Comics, 2007

Little Mouse Gets Ready! (Written and drawn by Jeff Smith, color, sc and hc). Toon Books, 2009

"Mad scientist" in *The Best American Comics 2011*. Houghton Mifflin Harcourt, 2011.

Bone The Great Cow Race Artist Edition (b&w, hc). IDW, 2013

The Best American Comics 2013. Editor with Jessica Abel and Matt Madden. Houghton Mifflin Harcourt, 2013.

CONTENTS

INTRODUCTION

JEFF SMITH'S EPIC JOURNEY

Jeff Smith was born February 27, 1960, in small-town western Pennsylvania then raised in Columbus, Ohio. From these modest origins, Jeff Smith rose up to be one of the great comics creators of our time. First with his magisterial epic, *Bone* (translated into over twenty-four languages), followed by his mind-bending, time-warping sci-fi noir *RASL,* the Paleolithic-set fantasy *Tüki: Save the Humans,* his art-house styled superheroic mini-series, *Shazam!* (with DC), to his latest children's book, *Smiley's Dream Book* (2018).

Of course, Smith didn't become the giant he is today ex nihilo. Already at a young age, he began systematically honing his word-drawing skills. As a child, Smith was inescapably drawn to how Charles Schulz (*Peanuts*), Carl Barks (*Donald Duck*), and Walt Kelly (*Pogo*) could create richly rendered anthropomorphic storyworlds where careful line work conveyed complex interactions, actions, and interior states of mind that triggered a wide range of thoughts and feelings in readers. Already as a child, then, Smith began the daily practice of drawing of his own stories. As Smith grew, so too did the cultural phenomena broaden and widen in his education as an artist. The way Franco-Belgians like Peyo (*Smurf*) and Hergé (*Tintin*) as well as Jack Kirby (*Fantastic Four*), and Neal Adams (*Batman* and *Green Lantern*) could use different line-work styles, perspective, framing, angles, and layouts convey all variety of meaning; how they could use drawing and words to create narratives that would radically alter the way readers would apprehend the world.

This education continued with Smith's discovery as a teen of the underground comix scene, especially those published by Kitchen Sink such as the first two issues of Will Eisner's *The Spirit;* Eisner showed Smith what could be done to convey meaning with the deft handling of thick and thin ink-lines as well as how the careful placement of large panel insets could bend time and space. And, with a whole variety of comics from all genres, worldly traditions, and earlier epochs filling up headshops and comic book stores, Smith could more formally study the likes of George Herriman's *Krazy Kat,* Carl Barks's *Uncle Scrooge,* Joe Kubert's *Sgt. Rock* and *Tarzan* as well as creators like avant-garde, epic sci-fi graphic mythologists like Moebius, Enki Bilal, and Alejandro Jodorowsky, whose work he could find in the magazine *Heavy Metal*—the US licensed version of the French *Métal Hurlant.* Smith was a big reader, too, of those weighty alphabetic narrative tomes like *The Odyssey, Don Quixote, Huck Finn, Moby Dick,* and *Lord of the Rings.*

For the young Jeff, these worldly creators and others showed him how to pace stories, expand time and space, as well as create dreamscapes where anything could happen. They showed him how words and visual art could create storyworlds that made new his perception, thought and feeling about the world.

He knew he wanted to hone the word-drawing storytelling arts, so he applied and got into The Columbus College of Art and Design—with a scholarship. However, this was during the period in the early 1980s when such art colleges were either for those who wanted to become commercial artists or those who wanted to train as fine artists. Smith wanted to sharpen his skills as a comics creator—and learn as much as possible about how to create animation (along with cartoon strips and comics, as a child Smith was mesmerized by Disney's animations). He knew that if he transferred to the Ohio State University, that he might get a chance to draw a comic strip for its college paper, *The Lantern.* He transferred and in 1982 began creating the comic strip, *Thorn,* for *The Lantern.* This and the tremendous collections of comics growing rapidly at OSU's Billy Ireland Cartoon Research Library became Smith's curriculum of study; he never quite found his footing with journalism and art.

With years of experience writing *Thorn* under high-pressure deadlines for *The Lantern,* Smith knew he could pull this off on a larger scale. He tried to catch the eye of the newspaper syndicates. He sent his *Thorn* strip to every syndicate out there, including Tribune Media Services and King Features. They all turned him down. Fortunately, there was a sea-change about to happen in the world of comics in the US. 1986 saw the publication of game-changers such as *Maus, Dark Knight Returns,* and *Watchmen.* This revolution in format showed Smith another way to get his comics out into the world: as books with big story arcs. And, he was equally inspired by Ben Edlund's success with self-publishing his satirical superhero comic, *The Tick.* Smith realized he didn't need the syndicates. He could create a story world that he could grow on his own—and into something much bigger.

The comics marketplace had yet to catch up to this revolution in format. While Spiegelman and Miller were making big comic books, the comic book stores during this period weren't on board—at all. The comics industry generated its profits in the selling of single-issue comics coveted by readers; with prices inflated wildly by publishers (small-print runs) and comic book stores (no restocking) working together to drive prices higher for these rare single-issue comics. The marketplace wasn't quite ready for what would eventually become Smith's *Bone*.

This didn't stop Smith from continuing his education as a visual storyteller. With Jim Kammerud and Marty Fuller, Smith started the Columbus-based animation studio, Character Builders Inc. Smith learned by making animations and claymations for local businesses, animated sequences in feature films, and the opening to the TV series, *Super Safari with Jack Hanna*. Smith also learned first-hand how labor-intensive, unrelenting, and unforgiving the animation filmmaking business was. He sold his stake in the company and, in 1991, with life-partner and business partner, Vijaya Iyer, Smith launched his publishing company, Cartoon Books. This would prove to be one of the best decisions of his career.

The founding of Cartoon Books as the publishing platform for Smith to create his comics in short-book *and* single-volume format couldn't have come at a better time. The industry was taking a nosedive. Comic book stores were closing left and right. The artificial inflating of the comics sales bubble had burst.

Smith knew that if he published his comics as books, they would not only have a longer shelf life, they would have a better chance of being embraced by acquiring librarians across the country. Iyer and Smith knew that by selling his comic stories in book format with carefully organized mini-story arcs that would build into a major story arc, they would not only survive but thrive. They were right. When they launched the *Bone* series in 1991, it became so successful that Smith was quickly overrun with sales demands. So Smith could focus on the creating, Iyer left her Silicon Valley job to run the business as the President of Cartoon Books. While *Bone* was off to a quick and furious start, by the mid-1990s the comics industry hit rock bottom.

Bone was doing phenomenally well, including sweeping up the big comics industry prizes like the Eisner and Harvey Awards. It was doing well with libraries too. The success of *Bone* was enough for Smith and Iyer to get Image Comics to house it, without relinquishing rights and control. Image Comics came on board and published *Bone* issues 21 through 28, helping Smith and Iyer weather the storm. They took full control once again with issues 29 through 55. In 2004, Cartoon Books published a limited run, 1,332-page, one-volume edition of *Bone;* it picked up an Eisner for Best Graphic Album Reprint in 2005. And, this same year, Scholastic Inc.'s new kids comics imprint, Graphix, reissued the volumes in full color. Iyer and Smith brought on board colorist Steve

Hamaker to handle these coloring duties. In 2006, to hit up the UK markets, HarperCollins published *Bone* also in these full color editions.

During the 2000s, Smith's *Bone* continued to get lots of attention from readers, librarians, reviewers, and awards committees. This was the period of a renaissance in comics, this time in the form of books sold in bookstores like Barnes and Noble and Borders; most of these bookstores had dedicated sections to graphic novels—and manga, a suddenly hugely popular genre and format with readers. *Bone* had already found its readers, older and younger. And, during this period there was a massive uptick in requests not just for *Bone* at libraries, but graphic fiction and nonfiction generally. More publishers decided to jump into the game: Penguin with *Babymouse* (2005); Scholastic established its Graphix imprint (2005); the megalithic distributor Diamond launched Diamond Kids in 2006; ABRAMS established its kids imprint, Amulet Books, that would later publish the runaway success *Diary of a Wimpy Kid* (2013); and in 2010 Macmillan acquired First Second Books to gain more presence in the teen market. In 2012, to honor children's and YA comics, the Will Eisner Awards committee offered three new categories in these areas.

It's worth noting, too, that with the limelight shining on *Bone* there were also some detractors. For instance, library patrons in Minnesota tried to get it banned because of Smith's depiction of some characters smoking cigars and drinking alcohol. He was in good company; others in pockets across the country tried to ban Alison Bechdel's *Fun Home* and Satrapi's *Persepolis*. To this day, *Bone* remains in the top ten banned books for most number of complaints from schools and library patrons.

That Smith and Iyer decided to go the serial book and volume route paid off. Since its publication, *Bone* has picked up major accolades, including ten Eisner Awards and eleven Harvey Awards. By publishing it in hardback book form, it would fare better with library use. Already by 2002, it had become one of the most requested books across the country. It continues to be a favorite book among librarians and patrons.

The publishing of *Bone* in serial book format influenced storytelling technique. Already before setting ink to paper, Jeff knew that the *Bone* story would have a massive arc. He also knew that he had to pay bills, so waiting for the 1,300 behemoth that *Bone* would become wasn't feasible. He had to create chapters to form books with their own mini-arcs. And, these books would take about a year to create, so he had to figure out a way to keep his readers going while waiting from one book to the next. That is, he had to balance growing his readers with creating installments and with the creating of the big epic story. (This is also something we see in the careers of Jaime and

Gilbert Hernandez in their groundbreaking 1980s *Love and Rockets*—a series greatly admired by Smith.)

In many ways, the vision and execution that Smith brings to *Bone* is a model for understanding the major comics series he created afterwards. So, let me pause briefly in this story of his education as an artist to discuss in some detail the shaping devices he used in the creating of *Bone*.

At its most foundational, we see with *Bone* Smith's juxtaposition of different ontologies: the human world and that of the anthropomorphic Bone cousins world. Smith's visual and verbal techniques allow for the seamless integration of these otherwise disparate ontologies. In other hands, the realism of the adult world and the more iconic cartoon style of the Bone cousins would create hesitation in readers. However, Smith's epic-dimensioned plot and word-drawing archetypal characterizations (human and anthropomorphic alike) provide the narrative structures to welcome then guide readers into an immersive experience that makes no distinction nor discriminates between animal and human ontologies.

The reader's seamless imaginative movement between different ontologies is no easy feat. Think about those films like *Who Framed Roger Rabbit* and *Space Jam* that tried to do this, but failed precisely because the narrative shaping devices used caused audiences to hesitate in their imaginations as they moved from animated anthropomorphic bunnies to human actors. Smith pulls this off by creating a robust narrative—an epic on the scale of Melville's *Moby Dick;* by naming one of the rat cubs, Bartleby, Smith includes a signpost to indicate this for his readers. At the same time, as the narrative unfolds we see the building into the story an anything-goes Tex-Avery sensibility; in action and dialogue, the Bone cousins are without the types of restrictions (social and physical) seen with the human characters: they can do things that defy the laws of gravity and say things that transgress social taboos. And, Smith's minimalist line work and geometric shaping of the Bone cousins as more cartoony and iconic, by convention guide the reader to this anything-goes space. Stylistically, the Bone cousins stand in contrast to Jeff's use of the more rigid, *ligne-claire* detailed visuals of the human and natural world: Thorn, Gran'ma Ben, and the residents of The Valley, for instance. However, as mentioned already the epic-dimensioned narrative envelope allows the reader to seamlessly fit in their minds these two worlds together. This capacious envelope also allows Smith to take readers from a linear story where there's a clear sense of cause and effect into moments that are governed by the *illogic* of dreamtime; Thorn's movement between the waking and dreaming worlds is a case in point. I would argue, too, that Smith's capacity to have readers move seamless between these different registers and ontologies is why *Bone* has such a wide appeal: to children and teens as well as adult lay-readers and comic-book heads.

As I mentioned already, we see this same creative impulse—to seamlessly juxtapose ontologies, states of mind, time and space—in his other major comics series. In *RASL* (2008–2012) we certainly encounter some visual stylistic shifts: more horizontal panel layouts and no cartoony characters like the Bone cousins, for instance. However, Smith's building of the narrative foundation on a mythic re-dimensioned Nikola Tesla allows Smith to invite readers into an immersive, time-space bending experience; we not only move between parallel worlds, but because of Smith's deft geometrizing of story and character, readers will not hesitate when encountering the lizard-face (literally) assassin, Salvador "Sal" Crow in worlds only populated by human shaped characters. And, as we see in *Bone* the characters themselves never hesitate between these different ontologies. For *RASL,* encountering a human character like Maya or Annie is just the same as a character with a lizard face. Again, the strength of the foundational narrative along with Smith's careful line work and geometrizing of character and landscape allow for the reader to move seamlessly between these different ontologies.

Smith pulls off the same trick in *Shazam!: The Monster Society of Evil* (2007) where he innovatively reimagines Earth's Mightiest Mortal as a superhero whose complex personality is shaped as a result of the constant cross-generational influence of the young Billy with the adult Shazam. And, we see this same epic-narrative making and geometrizing of story in his webcomic, *Tüki: Save the Humans* (2014; 2015 as a print comic). Again, Smith's building of a story on epic-dimensioned foundations along with his capacity to move between maximal and minimal iconic styles clear a path for readers to imagine a world where cartoony anthropomorphic monkeys interact with our prehistoric ancestors: homo habilis *and* homo erectus. In these and his children's books, *Little Mouse Gets Ready* (2009) and *Smiley's Dream Book* (2018), we see Smith create foundational narratives with iconic and realist visual styles where readers move seamlessly in their imaginations between different ontologies.

Smith's word-drawn narratives powerfully engage readers of all ages and all variety of comic book experience. In addition to the techniques mentioned above, I would like to emphasize that Smith's hand drawing of all his comics and children's books adds to the kind of all-ages intimacy that the stories invite. Taken as a whole, we see too how Smith's visual-verbal narratives have significantly helped transform this narrative landscape. He made it okay for young readers to engage with epic-dimensioned, ethically complex stories. He made it okay for adult readers to experience transgressive pleasure and fun. He has helped clear space for scholars like myself to talk seriously about visual-verbal narratives that engage children and adults; we can dash aside those misconceptions that these narratives are somehow unsophisticated distant cousins to highbrow sanctioned literature and art. Finally, Smith's comics and creating of his successful Cartoon Books publishing company showed new generations of visual-verbal narrative creators that they, too, could make a difference. Jeff Smith's significant impact on the industry as creator and self-publisher cleared the way for the likes of Noelle Stevenson, Shannon Watters, Grace Ellis, Brooklyn A. Allen (*Lumberjanes* series), Raina Telgemeier (*Smile, Drama, The Baby-Sitters Club* series), Tim Fielder (*Matty's Rocket*), Tony Medina, John Jennings, Stacey Robinson (*I Am Alfonso Jones*), Gord Downie and Jeff Lemire (*Secret Path*), Sebastian Kadlecik, Kit and Emma Steinkellner (*Quince*)—even my own co-creation with Chris Escobar, *The Adventures of Chupacabra Charlie*. Smith's founding and directing of Cartoon Crossroads Columbus, which includes a generous award for best emerging comics artist, continues to open doors for future generations of comic book creators to own and successfully self-publish their work. For this and all else Smith remains an inspiration to us all.

FLA

CHRONOLOGY

1960	Jeff Smith is born February 27 in McKees Rocks, Pennsylvania, to William Earl Smith and Barbara Goodsell. At an early age, his family moves to Columbus, Ohio.
1978	Graduates from Worthington High School.
1979	Matriculates at Columbus College of Art and Design with a scholarship.
1982	Transfers to the Ohio State University. Begins creating his proto-*Bone* comic strip, *Thorn,* for college paper, *The Lantern.*
1984–88	Tries without success to nationally syndicate his strip, *Thorn.*
1986	Cofounds with Marty Fuller and Jim Kammerud (former high school and college classmates) the animation studio, Character Builders.
1991	With the help and support of his wife Vijaya Iyer, launches Created Cartoon Books and begins to publish his black-and-white comics series, *Bone.*
1993	Receives an Eisner Award for Best Humor Publication. To keep *Bone* in print and available, Smith collects the first six issues of the comic book into a graphic novel titled *The Complete Bone Adventures vol.1.*
1994	Publishes *Bone* issue 16 (October), an issue that is met with some controversy; the issue takes as long to read as the story unfolds. Some comic book fans don't like him experimenting with the form, and not sticking to a strictly cartoon-styled, fun story. Many think the near totally wordless issue did not have enough words to justify the cover price.
1994	Creates an original cover for Dan DeBono's *Indy: The Independent Comic Guide* (issue 13). Receives Harvey Awards in three categories: Best Cartoonist, Humor, and Best Graphic Album of Previously Published Work. Receives Eisner Awards in four categories: Best Serialized Story, Best Continuing Series, Best Writer/Artist, and Best Humor Publication. Dark Horse, Graphitti Designs, and others

begin releasing a series of *Bone* cold-cast statues. The November issue of the *Comics Journal* features a cover interview with Smith.

1995   Begins to publish *Bone* with Image Comics (issues 21–29); Image Comics also reprints the first twenty issues of the series with new cover art by Smith. Decides to reorganize the *Bone* collections (there had been three so far) into a series of volumes that highlight story-arcs. *The Complete Bone Adventures* volume one is retitled: *Bone Volume One: Out from Boneville*. Volumes two and three are also given subtitles.

Receives Eisner Awards in three categories: Best Humor Publication, Best Writer/Artist, and Best Continuing Series. Receives a Harvey Award for Best Cartoonist.

1996   Receives a Harvey Award for Best Cartoonist. Toy manufacturer Resaurus release *Bone* figures: Fone Bone, Smiley Bone, Rat Cub, and Thorn. Receives the Alph-Art at the Angouleme International Comics Festival for *Bone*.

1997   Receives a Harvey Award for Best Cartoonist.

1998   Receives Eisner Awards in two categories: Best Writer/Artist, and Humor.

1999   Receives a Harvey Award for Best Cartoonist.

2000   Receives a Harvey Award for Best Cartoonist.

2001   Smith and Vijaya travel to Kathmandu India to conduct research in the ancient city of Atheia; elements from this research weave themselves into Gran'ma Ben's former kingdom.

Cartoon Books continues the toy line, releases *Bone* figures: Gran'ma Ben, Phoney Bone, The Hooded One, and a deluxe-boxed set of Kingdok.

2003   DC Comics announces that Smith will write and draw a miniseries that recasts the Shazam origin story. Receives a Harvey Award for Best Cartoonist .

2004   Finishes the *Bone* story, publishing the final issue in May. In July, Cartoon Books publishes a single volume of the nine books that make up the *Bone* series, housing the complete cartoon epic in one 1,340 page tome.

2005   Scholastic launches their graphic novel imprint Graphix by publishing *Bone: Out from Boneville* in full-color. Portable, color versions of all nine *Bone* volumes are released over the next five years. Telltale Games releases video game, *Bone: Out from Boneville*.

Receives Eisner Award for Best Graphic Album Reprint *Reprint* for the *Bone One Volume Edition*, Harvey Award for Best Cartoonist, and Harvey Award for Best Graphic Album of Previously Published Work for the *Bone One Volume Edition*.

2006   Telltale Games releases video game, *The Great Cow Race*.

2007   DC Comics publishes Smith's *Shazam!: The Monster Society of Evil*. Designs the cover art for Say Anything's album, *In Defense of the Genre*. Dark Horse Comics Presents releases a new statue of Fone Bone as part of a series of famous characters. Sales of Scholastic's *Bone* reprints in color are in the millions.

2008   Begins serializing his sci-fi major comic series, *RASL*. The Ohio State University's Wexner Center for the Arts Museum curates the exhibit: "Jeff Smith: Bone and Beyond." Warner Bros. Pictures buys film rights to *Bone*.

2009   Documentary film released: *The Cartoonist: Jeff Smith, BONE, and the Changing Face of Comics*. Toon Books publishes Smith's thirty-two-page children's book, *Little Mouse Gets Ready*.

2010   A parent in the Rosemount-Apple Valley-Eagan School District in Minnesota tries to have *Bone* banned from all elementary school libraries, disturbed by the representation of characters smoking, drinking, and gambling. The school district voted ten to one to keep the book in its libraries.

2013   Smith, along with Jessica Abel and Matt Madden, coedit the *Best American Comics 2013*. Begins publishing his webcomic, *Tüki: Save the Humans*.

2014   Publishes *Tüki: Save the Humans* as a comic book. Receives an Eisner Award for the completed and colored *RASL* in the category of Best Graphic Album: Reprint.

2016   Smith, as President and Artistic Director, along with comic journalist Tom Spurgeon as Executive Director, create Cartoon Crossroads Columbus modeled after the Angoulême International Comics festival in France. Publishes thirty-six-page, *Bone: Coda* to celebrate the twenty-fifth anniversary of publishing *Bone*.

2018   Publishes the forty-page children's book, *Smiley's Dream Book, with* Scholastic. Cartoon Books publishes a paperback version of Smith's full color *RASL* story in three parts, *RASL: Book One: The Drift* (July), *RASL: Book Two: Romance at the Speed of Light* (Sept.), *RASL: Book Three: The Fire of St. George* (Nov.).

JEFF SMITH: CONVERSATIONS

A Short Interview with Jeff Smith

TOM SPURGEON / 1999

The Comics Reporter (December 31, 1999). Reprinted with permission.

Jeff Smith is one of my favorite people in comics, and I think his fantasy comic *Bone* is one of the medium's great surprises of the last quarter-century. I had the pleasure to interview Jeff once in late 1999 for a section of the "Trilogy Tour" issue of the *Comics Journal*. I remember I conducted the chat in Kim Thompson's office without a lot of preparation, but Jeff has a natural gift for speaking plainly about his work so the interview went very smoothly. The interview was conducted when he had crossed about the halfway point with *Bone*, but I think it was the first big one he did after his comic was revealed to be more of a fantasy than a humor book, like many people thought it was at first.

This was also the interview where Jeff talked about a confrontation with Dave Sim that led to Dave challenging Jeff to a fight, one of the odder sideshows in recent comics history, and something that makes me want to apologize to Jeff every time I see him.

What follows is my original introduction and the interview itself.

JEFF SMITH INTERVIEW

When Jeff Smith sat down and interviewed with Gary Groth in 1994, Bone was a different comic book being published in a different comics industry. What began as a Walt Kelly/Carl Barks-flavored humor strip has since become a straight-ahead grand fantasy, while the industry in which it's published has shrunk considerably. Smith is probably the last breakout success story of 1990s independent comics.

He has held his position admirably. Smith negotiated the worse part of the distributor implosion scare by aligning himself with a then-juggernaut Image Comics (at the same time exposing himself to a brand new fan base). Returning to self-publishing, Smith organized two Trilogy Tours of like-minded fantasy cartoonists and enjoyed the fruits of a successful, accessible property: foreign licensing, merchandise, and an eventual deal to write and direct a *Bone* movie from Nickelodeon films.

Smith's work has continued to accumulate Harvey and Eisner awards, and the cartoonist has cemented a reputation as one of the more accessible, easygoing professionals in the business. I interviewed him in October, following the conclusion of the second third of the *Bone* serial. Waiting for word from Hollywood to determine the length of his hiatus from *Bone*, Smith is keeping busy with two side projects set in his *Bone* "universe": drawing from Tom Sniegowski's script in *Stupid, Stupid Rat Tales* and writing for artist Charles Vess in the mini-series *Rose*.

HOW THINGS HAVE CHANGED

Tom Spurgeon: I have a feeling your workday is a little more complicated than it used to be.

Jeff Smith: Well, the days of just me by myself in my loft drawing the comic and packing the boxes for the UPS man, those days are gone. There's more things going on. I'm doing projects with other people; that's new for me. I'm working with Tom Sniegowski on *Stupid, Stupid, Rat Tales;* I'm writing a script for Charles Vess on Rose. We've got all sorts of other projects going on. We did *Bone* toys, all the foreign licensing. And a lot of travel. I still have to do a lot of moving around to promote the book.

Spurgeon: You were just in Europe, as I recall.

Smith: I just got back from Spain. *Bone* is doing very well in Spain. Number five on the pop charts there.

Spurgeon: Do you travel from a sense of business obligation, a feeling your work does well for you having made the trip?

Smith: Oh, yeah. I still do road trips to promote the book. I think that's the main difference between being a self-publisher and being at Dark Horse or something. There's no one out there reminding everyone that I'm still doing books. I have to go out and do that myself.

Spurgeon: How much of your day is dealing with the forthcoming animated movie? Is that now taking up more of your time?

Smith: No, not really. It's still pretty early in that process. In fact, now I'm not working on it at all. I finished a first draft of the script, and that's been at Nickelodeon for about two weeks.

Spurgeon: And what you're waiting on is a green light from them at which point you kind of make the transition over to doing that full-time?

Smith: Right.

Spurgeon: Do you have any idea what that entails? I know from your last comic you said you were going to put your comic on hiatus if the project was greenlighted.

Smith: No, I don't have any idea how I'm going to approach it, Tom. [*laughter*] It's Hollywood. It doesn't follow any known set of universal laws. It's its own thing. I'm not banking on it, I'm not trying to schedule around it. If it happens, great. Because I'm also an animator, you know? I'm really looking forward to doing it. But the process is completely beyond my control. I did as much as I could to make the situation the best that I could. But at some point, it's in Hollywood's hands. And I can't worry about that, because I'm not a Hollywood guy. I'm a comic book guy. If it works out, great, I'll go do that. If it doesn't, then fine. At this point, it really doesn't affect me either way.

Once we get a green light, okay, then I'll have to figure out what I'm going to do. What I'd like to do, hopefully, is have some decision by the first of the year. By then, I'm getting anxious to start *Bone* back up—the last part of *Bone,* the last fifteen–twenty issues or so. And I think by the first of the year, I want to know if I'm going to do that or if I'm doing the movie.

Spurgeon: You anticipate that being a hands-on process?

Smith: Yeah. I'll be directing it. And I'm writing it. So this first part of development was me writing this script with one of my old animators, who is a really good pal of mine.

Like I said, we just finished the first draft, gave it to Nick. Now if everything goes according to their liking, and we get the green light—I do think we'll probably know by the end of the year—then we'll go into preproduction. And I'm the director of the film at that point.

It'll be very hands on. I'll be doing tons of drawing, none of which will actually be on the screen, because I don't plan on doing any of the actual animation. But it'll be fun. I'm really looking forward to it. It's a kind of cartooning that's in my blood. Just as much as comic books.

BONE **THE BOOK**

Spurgeon: Speaking of comic books, when Gary interviewed you five years ago, *Bone* was a very different book. You were still in your early phase . . .
Smith: But, if you read that, I was telling you it was about to change.

Spurgeon: You dropped hints, and there are clues in the work as to your eventual direction, too—all sorts of portentous things happening. A couple of things that you say in that interview I wanted to ask you about. You said that the way you did the book originally, the lighthearted soap opera and comedy, was to establish a sense of place and a sense of the calm before the storm. You wanted to introduce the community that was ripped apart by the events of the fantasy. Do you think you were successful in doing that?
Smith: I think so. What I meant by that was that in order for anybody reading the story to care that there was some evil force trying to attack the town, you have to care about the town. That's one of the things that I see in bad knock-offs of Tolkien, or just bad sword-and-sorcery things as opposed to those that are more thought out. Anytime you have a bad knockoff, whether it's a knockoff or *The Dark Knight Returns,* or a knockoff of *The Acme Novelty Library*, people just pick up surface elements and they don't understand the underlying mechanisms that made the thing work in the first place.

In bad sword-and-sorcery, you get somebody on a quest, he picks up a friend, and they go fight this demon sorcerer guy and they're trying to save the world. But you don't care about the world, because you never met it.

So I thought it was really important to set up a place that we all like, that we all want to go. We know Gran'ma Ben, we know Lucius and his little cohorts in the town. We're familiar with them. And we like Gran'ma Ben's cabin, and we like the ridiculous adventures that go on. And that's what is taken away.

Spurgeon: Another thing you talked about was wanting to establish certain relationships between the characters. At one point, you actually told Gary one of the core points of *Bone* for you was the relationship between Fone Bone and Thorn. Which I guess has changed, but I'm not sure how to track that relationship. Could you talk about how that relationship has progressed?
Smith: I think if someone was looking for the consummation of their relationship, that's not the track I intended to take them on. It is one of the hardest things to track, because in all honesty I'm not sure where that relationship is at the moment.

But let me back up a minute. To me the relationship between Fone Bone and Thorn was very much like a crush, a high school type of crush, mostly on Fone Bone's part. And as far as consummating their relationship, I kind of think metaphorically that happened early on in the book. There's a couple of scenes where he's wildly in love with her, and she goes off to take a bath in the river while he's present, and drops her clothes off-panel. We don't really know what happens after that—and I don't think anything really happened after that—but that was the consummating of that relationship. That fills in for that need. And it's progressed now into a relationship that's more a partnership between them.

Their relationship still is the axis the whole book turns on. Even when they're separated from each other, one is always trying to find the other one. Even the final moment of that last chapter, when Thorn is lying on the ground, Fone Bone is the one who barrels down right through all the trouble to get to her. As far as romance . . . I'm not really sure where that's going. The whole story isn't scripted out that tightly. I do kind of picture bringing more of the romance back into Bone in the third section. All of the characters are back together again for the duration of the story.

Spurgeon: It occurs to me that Thorn is the one that changes, and *Bone* is in many ways about her self-discovery and her engaging her responsibilities. To look at what you said originally, that Fone Bone had a crush on her; it seems that there are parallels to how a relationship progresses past the crush phase, when you come into a full estimation of who the object of your love is, particularly as she becomes more formidable.
Smith: I think that's very . . . very good. [*laughter*]

That's kind of what I'm saying when I say it's progressed to the partnership stage. That's kind of what I'm trying to say. I've been involved in a relationship with my wife Vijaya for seventeen years now. And it's a very long, really powerful relationship. It progresses, it evolves, it's always changing.

I think . . . that what you said is very good. [*laughter*] I'll take it.

Spurgeon: Some of the character development . . . Smiley Bone is the one I don't get. [*laughs*] Is he just that character that resists any kind of character development?
Smith: I have no idea. I personally don't really understand Smiley myself. He's obviously comic relief in a book full of fools. [*laughs*] He sort of lives in the moment and takes pleasure anywhere. He's hedonistic, he's amoral, I don't see his character going on any arc, if that's what you mean. [*laughs*]

Most of the characters, even Phoney Bone, are traveling some kind of path that's going to take them through some kind of transformation. Smiley Bone—that will not happen to him. That's for sure.

Spurgeon: Is there something you're trying to say about friendship and loyalty with those characters?

Smith: Absolutely. Absolutely. That's one of the most important things in the world. What else is there in the world except for the friends that you have? There's nothing else going.

Spurgeon: Is there a situation within your own life where you've had to deal with an unrepentant scumbag like Phoney Bone? That seems to be the most interesting relationship these characters have, maintaining loyalty to Phoney despite the fact he does awful things over and over and over again.

Smith: Well, I've certainly met people like Phoney Bone, but I rarely maintain relationships with them. I usually put as much distance between myself and them as possible. But from a story point of view, he represents just one more aspect of a personality. And within all your friendships, everyone shifts around between those different types. Even with your best friend, you have moments where you just can't believe how whiny they're being. But you don't discard them.

Phoney's one redeeming quality really seems to be his loyalty. At any given point, he will sell out the universe, but if anyone suggests harm to his cousins, he turns right around on them. He says things like, "Say whatever you want about me, but watch your lip when you're talking about my cousins."

So yeah, loyalty is a really strong part of the story. It's really what it's all about, I think.

MISTER UNPOPULAR

Spurgeon: As it expands into a fantasy, it seems like you're working with thematic frameworks. There's an interesting discussion with Rockjaw and the Bones. He's lecturing them on nature and power as opposed to good versus evil. So you have Rockjaw's way of understanding the world, and you have the mystical understanding of the way the universe works the villagers maintain, and the practical western way the Bones have of seeing the way things work. Is this something you're trying to present, this idea of conflicting frameworks?

Smith: Absolutely. In fact, the whole Rockjaw part of the story—which was not very popular by the way. [*laughs*]

Spurgeon: Well, it's difficult. It very much increases the complexity of the story.

Smith: It increases the complexity, but it's presented as simply as I could. It's pared down to the point of almost being a video game: being chased, and just trying to get along a path to an end point. At the same time, I wanted to express certain ideas in the valley without having another scene of Gran'ma Ben sitting them down and explaining.

I thought what would be fun to do would be to explain these same philosophies from the viewpoint of children. Which in the Rockjaw story are the little orphans. There are all these orphans whose parents have all been eaten by rat creatures and they've all banded together to survive. They meet up with Fone Bone and Smiley Bone. From them, we learn their perspective on this mystical understanding. But to them, it's even more basic than what the valley people know. To them, it's almost instinct. It's what makes them start walking within minutes of being born, and knowing when to hide. Of course, for the humans, it seems a slightly more mystical thing that's involved in dreams and some other unseen forces.

Spurgeon: Is there something you're trying to work out with these competing—?

Smith: I'm not sure they are competing. I assume you're saying that this is competing with Rockjaw's philosophy. Rockjaw represents nature. His whole thing is he's trying to find out what side everybody's on, while it's never clear what side is he on. He represents a force of nature. And he says nature doesn't pick sides. Nature could care less about this or that, or whose Mommy was eaten by a rat creature. Nature doesn't care. And I think that does fit in with the underlying philosophy. The underlying philosophy of Bone is that it's up to you create your moral and philosophical base. It's up to you to decide who your loyalties are with, and to make the most out of life.

Does that make sense?

Spurgeon: That makes total sense. So that's the central theme of the larger story.

Smith: Very much so. Rockjaw, Master of the Eastern Border, as volume 5 of *Bone*, becomes the literal centerpiece of *Bone*. There are nine books and that's number five. It's also the philosophical heart of the story.

Spurgeon: Which came first, the philosophy or the character? Did you draw on amoral characters in similar stories? Did Rockjaw come from what you were reading, or to embody a certain moral point of view?

Smith: It's difficult to say [*laughs*] because I've been working with these characters for so long. I'm not really sure. There's a real mix of influences and early false starts on *Bone,* like the *Lantern* comic strip. After that . . .

A huge thing for me was Carl Sagan. His Pulitzer Prize-winning book was *The Dragons of Eden*, about the evolution of human consciousness. Sagan's idea is that with a primitive being, at the end of the brain stem you just have this little nub. As you get to a more evolved being, you get a slightly larger brain until you get to a human primate. And with each step of that is a closer—how do I explain this? You're one more step closer to the kind of consciousness we now experience. This kind of ties into Nietzche's idea that the way men walked in dreams—shit, I get this mixed up—what conscious life was to men a million years ago is the way we dream now.

Did you follow that?

Spurgeon: I gotcha.

Smith: [*laughs*] I obviously explained it very clearly.

Spurgeon: That's a hell of a lot for the last *Bone* books to follow through on. [*laughter*]

Smith: Right. It's been pretty well . . . it's not a totally new concept to the book. I think it's there. I think I know what the ending will be. But we will see. Because it does change as I go.

Spurgeon: Can you give me an example of something that's changed? Or something that's surprised you in the writing of it?

Smith: The dreaming itself, actually, was not exactly what I thought it was when I started out. It really was quite innocent the way it developed into what it became. I originally just wanted to do a flashback that wasn't a flashback. There were a couple of comic book conventions I didn't want to have in *Bone*: exposition boxes, I didn't want to have thought balloons, I didn't want to have flashbacks. If somebody's telling a story in *Bone,* you don't see a little bubble with their head up in the corner. I make them tell a story. If you're sitting around the campfire, you don't have a little projection screen there, you got to make people get into it with your words. So when I was trying to do backstory with Thorn, I came up with the concept of showing it in her dreams.

Pretty early on, I knew that the dreams were not just flashbacks, were not just dreams, they were some kind of suppressed memories for Thorn that were being shaken up by these weird Bone creatures coming into the valley. And the dragon was kind of playing everyone as pawns. Gran'ma Ben doesn't really want Thorn to know who she is, because she thinks it will be dangerous for Thorn and the valley. So she won't let the dragon get Thorn up and going, so he kind of uses the Bones to shake things up and rattle these repressed memories.

Then I started to have an understanding that most myths have some sense of these unseen forces. Whether it's Merlin in *Arthur,* or The Force in *Star Wars,* there's always some sense that there's more than we can see. And the dreaming just started to fill that role in *Bone.* And once it did, it became really clear to me what its role was. I always thought the unseen forces were there, I just didn't know how they were expressed or what they did. And boom, there they were. That caught me completely off guard.

Spurgeon: You wouldn't guess that by reading *Bone,* that that concept came late in the game.
Smith: It was within the original context of the story, but not that manifestation. So I'm glad to hear it's not a sore thumb. [*laughter*]

DRAWING

Spurgeon: Let's talk about some of the drawing you've done. It looks like the last issue was a lot of fun.
Smith: It was a blast. I think of myself more of the drawer than the writer.

Spurgeon: Really?
Smith: Yeah. That's the most fun.
I also thought that the last three issues you could really see I knew where I was going. I was having a ball, and it was all working. There have been issues where I'm in a really sticky spot, and I wasn't really sure exactly where I was going. And you can tell. The book looks strained. You can really see it. But when everything is working, man, I am like a locomotive with a full head of steam.

Spurgeon: The genius comic touch in that last issue was the appearance of the balloon.
Smith: I was really nervous about that. [*laughs*]

Spurgeon: This ridiculous Macy's-style balloon as a grim sign of prophecy . . . you were nervous doing that?

Smith: [*laughs*] I was terrified, terrified. But that's what *Bone* is. The thing I'm probably most well-known for is the "Great Cow Race," which is clearly one of the most ridiculous things ever done. I think on the one hand, it was completely the correct thing. Because that's what *Bone* is. *Bone* is this fantasy thing, it's all symbolism—if you want it. If you don't want it, you don't have to have it, either. *Bone* can work on this really surface level where it's just humor. I actually think the two levels work really well. Comedy is a great way to tell stories and entertain. It takes the edge off. *Bone* is just this—you know what it is. It's just this edgy version of a big fantasy story. I'm glad to have done [that sequence] too, because I think it will relax some people who were afraid that *Bone* was only taking itself seriously. It's really crucial that *Bone* doesn't take itself seriously. Because heaven knows I don't.

Spurgeon: Do you see this as a corrective, then? I don't remember a lot of knee-slapping hilarity in Tolkien's material, for instance. Does the seriousness of those kind of works bother you when you read them?

Smith: No, not necessarily. I just think it's my . . . [*pause*]

Spurgeon: Your contribution?

Smith: Well, possibly. Yeah. I'm not completely derivative of all my influences. [*laughs*] The best I can analyze where something ridiculous like this comes from is . . . In 1977, the summer before I was a senior in high school, somebody talked me into reading *The Lord of the Rings* for the first time. And that was the same summer *Star Wars* came out. And I believe that was the exact same summer that *Métal Hurlant* came over to the US as *Heavy Metal*. That's when I first saw it, anyway.

So in one summer, the summer of seventeen years old, I got Tolkien, *Star Wars*, and *Heavy Metal*. Moebius and Bilal. And it exploded my brain. There was so much there, and so much on idea levels, story ideas, on fantasy, on comics—I couldn't believe comics for adults. My whole life, my favorite things were *Pogo*, *Bugs Bunny*, *Uncle Scrooge*, which is really where the *Bones* come out of. So just to shovel all those things together made complete sense to me. I don't think I did sit down and—I know I didn't try to think, "This would be a great thing if you could balance comedy with serious stuff." I definitely didn't do that, to this day I don't try to create that way.

"SEND IT TO REWRITES!"

Spurgeon: You've reworked some of the *Bone* material. As I understand what you've told me, this began as a specific thing where there were pages you were dissatisfied with because your personal life had taken you away from the drawing table. Yet this is something you've continued doing.

Smith: Well yes, but not to the extent of that one part.

I do the comics, I get a reaction from my friends, and from people writing letters. And my own ability to read the comic book changes once it's in print. I have a pretty good ability to separate myself from the work, and act as my own editor in a sense, even when I'm working on it. As it gets to certain stages, where you've got pencils, I can sit down and read it as if I haven't written it. And I think that helps me keep *Bone* from just sinking into a cesspool of self-indulgence.

Spurgeon: So what brings you to re-doing a page?

Smith: It's when I don't get the reaction I was looking for. And the first time that really happened was when Gran'ma Ben revealed to Fone Bone and Thorn that she was not just this little peasant girl living out in the woods with her grandmother, but she was a hidden princess. And the reaction I got to that was not really very enthusiastic. [*laughter*]

Spurgeon: And you thought that was automatically a result of the presentation?

Smith: Yes. Well, there were two things. It could either be I didn't tell it very well, or the idea itself was flawed. [*laughter*] I didn't really feel like changing the idea. First of all, I didn't think it was flawed. I think that that's the story. That's what little peasant girls hidden away living in the forest with their grandmothers are. It's also what stories of transformation are about: the little hick farm boy goes into the big city and finds out he's the king.

I went back and looked at that part of the story, this was in *Bone #17*, and would have been reprinted in *Volume Three: Eyes of the Storm.* The original presentation was three pages of static shots of Gran'ma, Thorn and Fone Bone, sitting across a table in the cabin, with Gran'ma just talking to them. "Blah, blah, blah," just telling them this backstory, this explosion of backstory. [*laughs*] That's not a very good way to tell a story. That's certainly not a very good way to present a pivotal plot point.

There were elements I thought worked really well. I thought the moment where Gran'ma Ben stands up in front of Thorn and says, "Not only are you the princess of the land, but I was the queen at one time," and you can see a sense of Gran'ma Ben behind her as a young woman holding the sword and being a proud, Joan of Arc-looking character? I thought that worked really well.

Spurgeon: You like your big graphic moments.
Smith: Oh, yes.

Spurgeon: It's not an uncommon thing for you to take three-quarters of a page or even a full-page and do your big comic book moments.
Smith: I think pacing is extremely important in telling a story. You have six panels, bop bop bop bop bop, and suddenly I play with the size of the panels, without knowing it the reader becomes disturbed a little bit. Agitated. I don't think they should notice the panels have changed, but I think that they do. Something's going on. And then you hit 'em with a big splash panel.

Anyway, I just decided that in order to do that scene correctly, I shouldn't just have them sitting at that table. I needed to do lighting, have a little acting—have Fone Bone and Thorn interject into Gran'ma Ben's explanation, ask questions. It's just not in Fone Bone's personality to just sit there and listen to this big, expository paragraph that Gran'ma Ben's spouting out. So that's what I did. I went back and re-staged it. I gave it some mood, I put acting into it. And I think it turned out pretty well. Well, I'm satisfied with it; whether anyone else is, I don't know.

Spurgeon: And did anyone complain that you changed story elements between serialization and collection?
Smith: No, no.

Spurgeon: Are you done with it when it gets into the books?
Smith: Almost, almost. [*laughter*] I'm bad. We go back to press pretty often and that third one, the volume three, that's a third printing. I futzed with it even again just a little bit. Not too much. If I think it will make it better, then I'll make it better.

Spurgeon: You and I have talked about how this is really common to other art forms.
Smith: Absolutely. Playwrights will watch opening night with the audience. That's one of the most important rewrites that they do. I heard that in *West Side Story* they completely flopped two major scenes. The Officer Krupke scene in the final version happens early on when they're still innocent, before the

murder happens. Originally, that happened after the stabbing. Opening night, people were really confused by this light-hearted song.

And it's also not unheard of to rework things in comics. Hergé must have done *Tintin* stories over countless times until he's satisfied with them.

I think I do it because I care about the comics. I really want them to be really, really good.

NEW PROJECTS

Spurgeon: As much as the *Bone* story is a personal story for you, can you describe the impetus to do the two new projects? Are these as personal to you, or is this your art jones being satisfied? The "Big Johnson Bone" story, and the . . .
Smith: . . . "Rose" story.

Spurgeon: You're drawing the former and writing the latter.
Smith: Right.

It's a lot of different things. First and foremost, I needed a break with *Bone*. I was getting exhausted. We were doing so much: with the Trilogy Tour, with the toys, with movie contracts—they're a full-time job [*laughs*]—and *Bone* was reaching a critical, critical part of the story. One of my most favorite parts of the story. And it was exhausting. I was just like "I need to stop for a second. But I don't want to stop and drop off the face of the earth." Because that's what happens. I was trying to pull all sorts of things together.

So it's the end of a cycle, a big cliffhanger, end of Act II of *Bone*: it seems like that's a logical place for a brief intermission. Hopefully I can just deal with the movie people just enough to find out what's going on. The same time, I don't want to disappear. I wanted to make sure I stayed in comics, because that's really important to me. So I had a couple of ideas I'd been floating around with Tom and with Charles Vess we had talked about. Charles and I were just waiting for the identity of the hooded one to be made public—which was Gran'ma Ben's sister Briar—so that we could tell the story of young Rose and Briar in a prequel.

It seemed like it would be a good time for me to take a little break from *Bone*, but without stopping. Sort of like a working vacation. This is different for me. It's different working with Charles, and having all this knowledge of fantasy and story come flowing inward instead of just sitting down and working it all out myself and reading books on myths and things. All of the sudden I've got this other person who is really charging me up. And I can't even put into words how I feel about Charles' artwork. So that just gives me all sorts of new juices—

Plus I'm looking forward to writing and doing the layouts, and then I don't have to do the finished work! [*laughter*] Someone else can pull their hair out.

Spurgeon: It seems like if you're drawing on your fantasy background for the thing you're doing with Charles, and you're drawing on your Barks/Disney fascination with the Big Johnson Bone series. Is that fair?

Smith: That's completely fair. "Big Johnson Bone" is a lot like the early issues of *Bone*. It's really a lot more Barks. And yes, "Rose" is going to be much more like Tolkien. That's mostly because of the strength of the people I'm working with. Tom Sniegowski—in comics, for some reason, he's known as the guy who writes *Vampirella,* and as he puts it, "such diverse characters as Shi and Witchblade." [*laughter*] But he's actually one of the funniest people I ever met in comics. I couldn't believe he hadn't written a comedy. He did a backup story for *Bone,* the Riblit backup story, which was very funny, and I wanted to do something with him.

I can't remember the beginning of your question. Why am I doing this? The main reason is I wanted to take a break.

Spurgeon: The cynical supposition would be that this was a calculated effort on your part to broaden the franchise aspect of what you're doing. The snotty way to say it is that you now have three different properties to point to in your Bone Universe.

Smith: I think that's fair. If somebody thinks they can be snotty by pointing that out, that's fine. [*Spurgeon laughs*] With the movie contracts, any prequels I come up are part of the deal. So it doesn't actually benefit me to create them.

I'm not trying to franchise out to sell them. I'm just interested in the universe. One of the most important things to me about *Heavy Metal, Star Wars,* and *Lord of the Rings* was that there were these worlds, these fantasy existences that you can go to. I wanted to have the same thing. Tolkien created Middle-Earth, and you sure believed you could drop down suddenly in Middle-Earth and find a path and go meet someone. I wanted the same kind of thing in *Bone.*

FUN STUFF TO TALK ABOUT

Spurgeon: How are things going for you in the comics market now? How much is the comics market a percentage of your business?

Smith: My company is doing fine. *Bone* kind of settled down into twenty-five thousand right away after the big fallout. Just through the direct market.

Spurgeon: When is that exactly?
Smith: Just like a year or two after . . . you know . . .

Spurgeon: [*laughs*] There have been so many fallouts, Jeff, I have a hard time tracking which one.
Smith: When I talk fallout, I'm talking when Marvel bought Heroes World, December of '94, and things just collapsed. And I thought it was one solid collapse all the way up to . . .

Spurgeon: Capital being purchased by Diamond?
Smith: No, even now. I feel like we've possibly bottomed out. But I'm not thrilled with the attempts to get back up. Anyway, we settled into selling about twenty-five thousand an issue, and stayed that way with no drops the next three or four years. Also, my collections have gone through the roof. That first collection we've sold well over one hundred thousand. I would say that's ninety-five percent into the comic book market.

Spurgeon: Really?
Smith: Yeah.

Spurgeon: That's remarkable. The only other one hundred-thousand-selling books I can think of off the top of my head are Spiegelman's and McCloud's, and those were not comic store sales, as I understand it.
Smith: *Bone* is through the comic stores.

Spurgeon: Well over one hundred thousand?
Smith: Yeah. And according to Comics Retailer, volume six is still their best-selling trade paperback after only [*whispers*] Pokemon. [*laughter*]
  So my business is far and away concentrated on the comic book marketplace. That's by far where most of our revenues come from.

Spurgeon: Can you tell me why you hold that strategy? Because conventional wisdom says the opposite: the future is direct sales through the Internet, or through book stores. I know you're involved with those things, but why is the comics market so important to you?
Smith: Because I am involved with those things, and I know how much more the comic book store market buys. It's that simple. Vijaya and I have spent a lot of time in the last five years exploring every other market: foreign, licensing, bookstores, the Internet, and we're in all those places. Actually, we do very

well with the foreign editions. It's in thirteen languages, and it sells very well in all of them. But in the bookstores . . . we do okay. I wish we did a lot more. We do—actually, I don't know, I'd have to ask Vijaya. We get orders about once a week from Border's, Barnes and Noble, for a few copies. It should be a lot more, but it's not the way it works. And we've tried working with small publisher distributors, getting all the small publishers together—Fantagraphics probably works with someone like this.

Spurgeon: They do; I don't recall which one.

Smith: Somebody who can actually get a meeting with a buyer at one of the chains. And then the big book chain will buy 150 copies for all of Border's nationally. And it's like, "That's it?" And not only that, but I talked to our sales agent, and I said, "Look, *Bone* is a comedy or a fantasy. Get it racked with either of those. If people like *Calvin and Hobbes* or *The Far Side,* they might like *Bone.* And if they like *Lord of the Rings*, they might like *Bone*." The salesman would go talk to the buyer for any of these chains, and tell them that, and say this should go on the shelf with the humor books. And they'd go, "No, no, no. We know what this is. This is a comic book." They'd buy a small amount and they'd stick them—they still do—*Bone* in a little section with the *Dungeons and Dragons* games, and the rest of the comic books. All spine out, and all looking terrible.

We do very well in libraries. We sell a lot of *Bone* to libraries.

Spurgeon: Are you still frustrated by structural impediments in the comic book market?

Smith: Well, yes. I'm very unhappy with the exclusives that some companies cut with Diamond. They don't allow for any competition whatsoever. If you think of all the genres that exist, only one genre can ever be on the cover of our major catalog. The only catalog, really, we have. And it's always Spider-Man. Or Superman. "Look, Spider-Man's on the cover." It puts blinders on the whole industry, placing it on this extremely narrow path. I'm not happy about that at all.

I think that the exclusives came about as a way . . . it almost happened without anyone being able to control or stop it. People made really ridiculous decisions, everything just fell over and plopped into what it did. To be honest, I think those arrangements, in the early part of 1995, probably saved the industry from a complete collapse. But I think at this point it's strangling it, and it only supports the old way of doing things: selling superheroes to obsessive-compulsive collectors. I don't see that as healthy. At all.

Spurgeon: I thought of your going to Image again after you signed with Nickelodeon and the *Rugrats* movie came out and did extremely well at the box office. And I thought, "Jeff makes good choices." You have a reputation as a sort of sharp operator.

Smith: I don't know about that. I do know I separate my artwork from the business of the artwork. I don't think any of the turmoil that surrounded me, the comics industry, self-publishing, going to Image, I don't think any of that should show up or be reflected in the work itself. And I'm very sure that it isn't reflected in that work. You can read the six *Bone* collections right now, which is one story from the beginning, and it doesn't indicate when I went to Image, or when I left Image and went back to self-publishing. And all the rest of it is fun stuff to talk about.

The business part for me is to make sure I have enough money to do the rest of the *Bone* story. Period.

MEMBER OF THE TRIBE

Spurgeon: This is the Trilogy Tour issue.
Smith: We're going to talk about the Trilogy Tour?

Spurgeon: Linda Medley and Charles Vess are being interviewed in this issue. I was wondering how much of an effect it had on you to carve out your own mini-community in comics.
Smith: I hope you have a lot of tape ready. [*laughs*]

It was wonderful. Because I left one community very abruptly. The whole self-publishing wave or movement or whatever you call it sprung up so quickly and it was so spontaneous. And then it became this giant, wavy monster that had its own rules and bylaws and manifests. When I left that community, it felt like stepping off a moving train, and rolling a while on the rocks. [*laughter*]

Even Image, I didn't go to Image until almost three months after that. I think people connect those two events, like I just left self-publishing and went to Image.

Spurgeon: Well, I think you were kind of coy about the termination of your relationship with Dave Sim and the other self-publishers.
Smith: I was. A lot of the other self-publishers bombarded me with letters and phone calls saying, "Don't talk about it!" [*Spurgeon laughs*] And I was like, "Cool." I wasn't looking forward to talking about it. So I didn't.

Spurgeon: Is there anything you can say about that now?

Smith: There's not much to say about it. A lot of it is based around Dave's infamous *Cerebus #186* where he published his little "tract" about women sucking the life blood out of men, and how they couldn't think—there were just so many horrible things. He actually used my wife Vijaya and myself as characters in that little tract. That was unacceptable to me. He was crossing a line. And it wasn't a line that he hadn't been warned about crossing.

Spurgeon: He talked to you about it beforehand?

Smith: What he wrote about was a time he came to visit me, and he told Vijaya and me a story, he told us about his ideas. He sat down on the couch and said, "Let me tell you the color of the sky in my world." And then he talked about what he wrote about in #186. This completely upside-down world. Vijaya and I sat there, and at first we talked about it with him. We were like, "Wow!" And you go, "You kind of have a point there sort of, but it's upside-down there at the end." And he goes on for like two hours. Droning on and on. I almost felt like I knew what it was like to be in Waco with David Koresh. [*laughter*] On and on . . .

Spurgeon: Dave can talk.

Smith: He's going on and on and on, and Vijaya and I are like going, "Can we go to the bathroom now?" It was just so . . . he just wouldn't shut up. And finally I said, "Dave, if you don't shut up right now, I'm going to take you outside and I'm going to deck you."

Spurgeon: Really? Wow!

Smith: It was that serious. There was dead silence, and he squinted his eyes. He took a drag off his cigarette. And that was it. We had a fun time. We went down to the first year at APE (Alternative Press Expo). That's why he was in town. We went on to have a really nice weekend. We didn't talk about it again.

Then that issue came out, where he told that story. My God, it's one thing to drag out your crackpot theories in front of people, but to put them down in print, that was unbelievable to me. And then he told the story about myself and Vijaya it wasn't how it happened, and he portrayed me as some sort of terrified, housewhipped boy, [*scared voice*] "Vijaya, stop giving away the secrets of the universe. Stop giving them away. I'll get in trouble, Vijaya." He completely changed the end of the story, which was me about to give him a fat lip. [*laughter*]

To add insult to the injury, on the back cover of *Cerebus #186* he listed the Spirits of Independence tour show dates, when they were going to happen, in what city, and who was going to be there. The Spirits of Independence tour was something we had come up with—me, Larry Marder, Dave, and Martin Wagner were going to do a tour. We were working on a tour for a year and a half, and we were supposed to get together later that month and decide when it was going to be. But we were having a struggle over whether it was about self-publishing or whether it was about just creators. My whole deal was never self-publishing. My whole deal was creators who are driving the ship. That's all I care about. Dave's whole thing was it has to be self-publishing. He got real aggressive about it, and decided that the rest of us didn't really need to go on the tour. [*laughs*]

So the whole thing was just like . . . I just had it. I just had it. You're going around and you're telling people they're going to get rich, be the next *Bone*. And that was just not true. And the whole thing . . . I didn't want to have anything more to do with it.

Spurgeon: From that unhealthy relationship to the healthy relationships on the Trilogy Tour.

Smith: Exactly. Trilogy was everything that I wished had been in the self-publishing movement, and what I had originally envisioned for the Spirits of Independence tour. It was a group of like-minded creators banding together and just going around the country. It was much more healthy, much more productive, manner.

Spurgeon: Well, you had all the stable, nice ones with you. [*Smith laughs*] Every stable cartoonist was on one of those tours, and the rest of them are nuts.

Smith: That's right. And the second year, when we invited people to join us—Jill, Stan Sakai, and Mark Crilly—all very talented, very stable, and productive cartoonists. With self-publishing movement, you're talking about . . .

Spurgeon: Well, you just said you were working with Larry and Martin. Are there two less productive cartoonists in the history of cartooning?

Smith: Well, at the time they were energized and they had started some things. [*laughs*] I know. Larry kills me. It's [*Tales of the Beanworld*] truly one of my favorite comics of all time, and it's heartbreaking that he's not producing them. But he'll surprise us. Someday.

The serious answer is that I really found a happy place . . . well, that sentence is going nowhere. [*laughter*] I was really happy once I started doing the tour with Charles and Linda. We had a lot of fun; we put a lot of energy into it. It was a massive, expensive undertaking. But it achieved everything we wanted to do. It gave us an identity. It really helped Linda—she was so ready to be discovered. And it was just going to happen. My whole memory, anyway, is that it was Linda's idea to start banding together. She just hooked up with the right guys. [*laughs*] Charles designed that tree . . . Man, those are the two best years in comics that I can remember. It was phenomenal.

Jeff Smith

TASHA ROBINSON / 2000

The A. V. Club (May 31, 2000). Reprinted with permission.

Jeff Smith is one of independent comics' greatest success stories. Since its 1991 debut, his quirky, charming, self-published fantasy series *Bone* has evolved from an obscure cult hit into a cottage industry, published in thirteen languages around the world. The epic story of three blobby, marshmallow-like creatures called "Bones" lost in a richly detailed world of hideous monsters and cute Disney-esque creatures, has won Smith dozens of awards—including, most recently, his sixth Harvey for Best Cartoonist. Smith put the *Bone* comic book on hiatus in 1999 to write, direct, and produce a theatrical animated adaptation planned for release this year. That film is still in development. Meanwhile, *Bone* returns this month, and Smith's company, Cartoon Books, is publishing its first non-*Bone*-related book, Linda Medley's fairy-tale-inspired *Castle Waiting*. Also in the works: a *Bone* prequel miniseries, *Rose*, written by Smith and illustrated by *Ballads And Sagas* artist Charles Vess. Smith recently spoke to the *A. V. Club* about his history and Hollywood physics.

Tasha Robinson: Is it true that you had the original idea for *Bone* in kindergarten?

Jeff Smith: Yeah, but it wasn't the full-blown idea. It was these three little Warner Bros./Disney-type characters who had adventures in their little world. They had relationships with each other that are pretty much the same relationships they have now. So I guess the characters themselves, even in kindergarten, were pretty full-blown. I had Fone Bone, who was the good, patsy-type leader for his other cousins; Phoney Bone, his cousin who was greedy and self-centered; and Smiley Bone, who was the happy-go-lucky ne'er-do-well. I can look at those old cartoons I drew when I was, like, eight, and their personalities were intact, even then.

Robinson: Did you always want to be a cartoonist?

Smith: Yeah, I did. I mean, you're five, so what do you know? But I loved Woody Woodpecker, I loved Mickey Mouse, I loved Bugs Bunny, and I knew that all these characters had a creator: I knew Walter Lantz made up Woody Woodpecker, and I knew Walt Disney made up Donald Duck. And I did want to have my own characters. So I doodled around and made up all sorts of them. I think all kids do. All kids draw some kind of cartoon characters. They just grow out of them, and I didn't. [*Laughs.*] And for some reason, the Bones were the ones that stuck with me. Out of all the ones I used to draw as a kid, those were the ones that kept reappearing absentmindedly in the margins of my school papers, climbing up the blue stripes that you're supposed to write on, then falling off again and crashing to the bottom of the page.

Robinson: Did you actively pursue a cartooning career when you were young? Do you have any formal art training?

Smith: Not really, although I had a very good teacher in high school who pushed me toward art school. I'm not sure I had any clear idea of where I wanted to go. I attended the Columbus College of Art & Design for a little while, until I realized they didn't take cartooning very seriously. Then I ended up going to Ohio State, where they had a daily newspaper and I could draw a comic strip every day of the week. I thought, "Now, that's some useful training. That's something I could do."

Robinson: Those strips for *The Lantern* look very similar to *Bone*, with the same cast and even some of the same jokes. Your artistic style has been consistent over the years.

Smith: It was definitely an early false start on *Bone*. I knew I had these characters, but I didn't really know exactly what I wanted to do with them. They're funny, and they're Bugs Bunny-like, but the stories I'm interested in are longer adventure stories. I made a few attempts: *The Lantern* one was an attempt to do a fantasy situation, but with a daily *Doonesbury*-type comic ending, which got mixed results at best. [*Laughs.*]

Robinson: Have you considered publishing those early strips?

Smith: I did collect them once. I put them in a little book when I was still in school, and I sold those around campus. I went to a printer, published it, and physically carried it around to all the different bookstores in Columbus. I sold two thousand of them, and I'd only printed 2,500. But, boy, I can't stand looking at them now. I look back at them and they're just horrible. They're so . . . so . . . I have no desire to print them again at all.

Robinson: What was your major at OSU?
Smith: I never graduated, but I was kind of floating between journalism and art because neither one wanted to claim me as a cartoonist. Cartooning is some kind of bastard child of art and journalism.

Robinson: When you left college, you helped found the Character Builders animation studio. Did you ever consider using the studio to independently animate *Bone?*
Smith: I wondered if I could do an independent *Bone* thing, a short or something. It was pretty vague, I was young, and I didn't know what I wanted to do with the story or my characters. But as I got into the animation, as I learned more about the business, I learned that you need a lot of people to do anything animated—even a short, let alone a feature film. And you need a lot of money. So you need to convince a bunch of people to do this idea, to let you be the director and to give you millions of dollars, and I started to think, "I don't know how feasible that is. It might make more sense to do it in print." Which was my original childhood love anyway, stuff like *Peanuts* and *Doonesbury.* So I started to look into going back into print cartooning, and I discovered *The Tick,* by Ben Edlund, which was a self-published comic book. That led me into comic-book stores. I had no idea that there were stores all over the world that sold comic books, and that there was a distribution process where you could set up your own label and get your books on the shelves. Once I did that, I could suddenly do the world of *Bone,* and I discovered this canvas that was perfect for telling it. It pulled me away from animation instantly.

Robinson: At one point, you did intend to publish *Bone* as a mainstream newspaper comic strip, right?
Smith: That was what I originally wanted, yes. The syndicates were smart enough to see that it didn't belong there. I spent a couple of years developing it, first with Tribune Media Services and then with King Features, but in the end it just didn't fly for a number of reasons. Mostly it wasn't funny enough. Like I said, it didn't belong in a comic strip. It's this fantasy world and an ongoing adventure, and a continuity strip today just isn't the same nowadays as it was when you had stuff like *Flash Gordon* and *The Phantom.*

Robinson: When you did the first issue of *Bone*, how much of the overall story had you planned out?

Smith: I thought I had a pretty good idea, and I did. I knew the ending, and I had a large, broad outline all set up. I made sure I wrote the ending, and I wrote the last page before I sat down and drew the first page.

Robinson: How much spontaneity goes into the individual issues?

Smith: A huge amount. That big giant broad plan is a wide road that I can wander all over. I find that the best moments come completely unexpectedly. I'm probably best known in comics for doing this segment called "The Great Cow Race," which is Gran'ma Ben racing, on foot, against all these cows. It's a really ridiculous, stupid thing, and it was not in the big outline at all. Gran'ma Ben was just this little, crazy old lady who raced cows. I thought that was sort of an off-the-top, *Far Side*-type joke. She's just weird. But then I started getting letters from readers saying, "Oh, I can't wait to see Gran'ma race the cows! I can't wait for the big cow race!" And I thought, "Oh, my gosh, I've created this expectation!" I could see in the story that I was sort of pulling toward it. The readers knew I was going toward it and I didn't. So eventually I had to belly up to the bar and put a cow race in the story. It turned out really well, and I fooled everyone.

Robinson: Did you deliberately start with a funny story to draw people in and then shift tones once you had an audience, or have your intentions for *Bone* evolved over the last decade?

Smith: That was actually very intentional. Even now, when we're working on the movie and we're working on scripts, I have to keep reminding everyone that you don't just jump to the fantasy. I think people have a little wall they throw up real quick if they see swords and sorcery. There's some really schlocky swords and sorcery out there, some schlocky fantasy. Even if a new TV show comes on and it's really good and everybody's trying to get you sucked in, you don't want to watch it at first. You're like, "I don't have time to get into one more big thing. I don't want to have to watch that new TV show every week." It's the same thing with comics or fantasy. If I'd started *Bone* and said, "This is going to be a giant epic," people would be like, "Do I really want to get into that?" So I intentionally backed up and said, "I'll start with just the Bones, with simple Disney-and Uncle Scrooge-type adventures. We'll just proceed and let the characters fall into the adventure, just the way you fall into your adventures in real life.

Robinson: How has the writing process changed for you as the plot has gotten more complex?

Smith: Well, it's become more difficult. I have so many balls in the air that I have to constantly go back, reread, and say, "Oops, I almost forgot about that one; gotta tie that up." That was one of the main reasons I took the break, even more than working on the movie. It just all kind of came together at the same time. I'd reached this point at the end of Act Two where I'd pulled all these threads together and it was something. It's a really big story, and I'd had no idea how big the story had gotten. Even I still look at *Bone* and think of it as a pretty simple little story, but it's massively complicated. I needed to step back from it for just a second, because that constant deadline of putting that book out every two months . . . You get to a point where you don't have time to think. That can be good, because sometimes when you don't have time to think you get some unexpected flow-of-consciousness stuff in there, but I needed to step back, reassess the whole story, and make sure it's on track the way everything's going.

Robinson: The story has gotten more sophisticated, but some people probably still look at the simply drawn characters and the slapstick humor and assume it's a children's comic. Do you write it for any particular age group?

Smith: I'm not sure. I think I write it for me. I know that might sound like a cliché, but I'm pretty sure there are other people like me who are adults . . . I'm forty years old, and I still love watching Bugs Bunny slap the bull on the nose. I still watch those cartoons, and yet I also enjoy reading books about science, or the current fiction. I think the audience is truly all ages: I don't put anything in there that kids can't see, or shouldn't see, but I have to keep it interesting for me as an adult. I'm not sure who the audience is; I'm just glad they're reading it.

Robinson: Your love of cartoons shows in your sense of comic timing.

Smith: Oh, yeah. I'm not sure exactly how it all works, of course. I do know that I look at the world of *Bone* as one that's in motion. I don't think of it as a separated-out, drawn-frame-by-frame comic. I think the characters are really moving. When I want to set the timing up, I try to make it look like the frames are just little boxes up above that we're looking through into the world, and they just have to move. So the timing has to be the same comic timing you would have comic actors use. It's not funny if it doesn't snap, you know?

Robinson: The motif of a highly detailed background and iconic, cartoony characters is common in Japanese and independent American comics, but it's not seen nearly as much in the mainstream. How did you arrive at the style?

Smith: It definitely wasn't conscious. I think it was because the comics I loved were *Tintin*, which is a little round-headed boy with a little swoop of hair, and totally realistic backgrounds, with absolutely authentic detail in every background. *Uncle Scrooge* by Carl Barks. This duck wearing spats and a top hat dives into his money bin, and every single coin is lovingly rendered. Or the bulldozer he uses to move the money around: Every nut and bolt is perfect and real. I actually think that kind of reality in the backgrounds adds to the believability of the comic as a whole.

Robinson: Scott McCloud's *Understanding Comics* talks a lot about the reasoning behind that style. Did you feel a spark of recognition when you read it?

Smith: Exactly. My whole take on *Understanding Comics* was like, "Wow, I kind of knew all this stuff, but this is like pulling away the curtain when I could just see the shapes through it." I enjoyed *Understanding Comics* quite a bit.

Robinson: Some press releases from 1999 indicated that you were taking two years off for the *Bone* movie, but the current reports make it look like bringing the comic back this year was the plan all along.

Smith: I've found that in Hollywood there is no "plan all along." They don't operate under the same rules of physics as we do. I think we were a little optimistic: We thought that, because *Bone* was so fleshed out, our development time would be really short, like six months or so. Instead, it's turned out to be a fairly normal development time of two years. But things are going really well, and we're hoping to put the movie out in 2002. But I didn't want to take any more time from my real field, which is comic books.

Robinson: Now that you're back to doing the comic book, have you changed your mind about directing the movie yourself?

Smith: I won't do the *Bone* comic once I start directing full-time.

Robinson: The comic will go back on hiatus? When?

Smith: I have a foggy timeline. It'll be around September or October so I can put out a couple of issues of *Bone*. I'm trying to balance it. I don't know. The movie could take a longer or shorter amount of time. It's hard to say.

Robinson: What's the sticking point with the movie? Why the delay in production?

Smith: Nothing, really, just the normal course of putting it together. We're working on the script. I just turned in a draft before Christmas, and that got the go-ahead to go to the next level. So now we're doing a rewrite that's happening right now. When that's done, hopefully we start.

Robinson: How has the plot of the movie evolved with the rewrites?

Smith: Now it's looking like it's going to follow closer to the comic than my first draft actually did, and go from the beginning through the "Dragonslayer" storyline, where Phoney Bone whips up the villagers' fears and superstitions about dragons for his own benefit. Sort of a McCarthy-era thing, where anyone who doesn't agree with Phoney gets labeled a dragon sympathizer. I think that's where we're going to take the story. I'm really happy with the direction of it right now.

Robinson: Have you considered voices at all?

Smith: No, I haven't. I'm terrified of that part. [*Laughs.*]

Robinson: What if you could get anyone you wanted?

Smith: Just a fantasy wish list? Okay, for Fone Bone, Tim Robbins. He's such a great actor, but all his acting comes from inside. Maybe Danny DeVito for Phoney Bone. Smiley Bone? I'm not sure. Bill Murray might not be bad. A really good suggestion somebody made to me was for the dragon: Tom Waits.

Robinson: What about Gran'ma Ben and Lucius? Thorn?

Smith: I just can't picture it. I'm terrified.

Robinson: Are you a big *Moby Dick* fan? Is that how it keeps finding its way into *Bone?*

Smith: Oh, yeah, I'm a huge *Moby Dick* fan. And you don't want me to talk about it. [*Laughs.*]

Robinson: Are the running gags, where Fone Bone talks about *Moby Dick* and everyone falls asleep, taken from personal experience?

Smith: Oh, yes. Sigh.

Robinson: Is this upcoming story arc going to be the end of the *Bone* series?

Smith: Yes.

Robinson: What will you do after that?

Smith: I don't know. It'll take me between three and five years to do the last three large books, and I can't think past that. I do have another project coming up with Paul Pope. He's one of my dearest friends in comics and one of the best cartoonists working today, I think. He's known for doing these oversized books, and we're going to do one together. It's going to be called *Big Big*, and we're each going to do a self-contained forty-page science-fiction story in it.

Robinson: Have you started work on it yet?

Smith: We're still talking. We're pretty much committed to the idea, but we're not sure what the plan is. We had talked about 2001, but we're still in the planning stages. But it's fun. That's something I want to do before *Bone* ends, so I can do stuff like that after it ends.

Robinson: Have you ever considered doing a comic about Boneville itself?

Smith: Not really. Maybe in the beginning I did, but once I started getting feedback in the letters . . . That's the interesting thing about doing comic books that come out as a serial: Every time an issue comes out, there's this communal discussion of the issue on the Internet and in the letters, and it's a very different way of progressing in your story than just doing a novel and putting it out. I realized that everybody had their own vision of what Boneville looked like. It was their own little world that they had created, whether it was Duckburg or some fantasy place. I could never draw a Boneville that would match everybody's ideas, and maybe I shouldn't. Maybe I should just let everybody make up Boneville, and Boneville will just be something inside everybody. I decided, "Why don't I just leave it at that?"

Robinson: People often cite Walt Kelly's *Pogo* as one of your primary inspirations, partially because Fone Bone looks something like Pogo. Do you think the connections run deeper than that?

Smith: I think on a slightly deeper level I learned a lot from Walt Kelly about giving characters personalities, about making them personalities that talk to each other. I learned a lot from reading *Pogo* about how to make Albert sound like Albert, how to make Churchy sound like Churchy, how to make Phoney Bone sound like Phoney Bone and Gran'ma Ben sound like Gran'ma Ben, if you follow me. But beyond that, they're very different comics. Walt Kelly was much more interested in allegory and politics, and I'm much more interested in metaphors and myth.

Robinson: What would you like to do with *Bone* in the next five years that you haven't done so far?

Smith: Well, I need to wrap up the story. [*Laughs.*] And there's some good-fun-wow stuff coming. I mean, it's all building up to it. The only thing I'm dreading is that there's a lot of characters and a lot of the story ahead, so I've got to bring everyone together.

Robinson: If you could go back in time and talk to that kindergartner drawing *Bones* in the margins of his schoolwork, what would you tell him?

Smith: Erase it! Quick! [*Laughs.*] No, I think that little kid would be happier than a pig in shit. Because I'm still that kindergartner, and I'm still sitting here doing it.

Jeff Smith: The *Ain't It Cool* Interview

ALEXANDRA DUPONT / 2003

Ain't It Cool, July 4, 2003. Reprinted with permission.

So last November I was buying some *Bone* collections for my stepdaughter from the comic's official website. On a whim, I asked the woman helping me with my order if series creator Jeff Smith would consent to an AICN interview.

As a matter of fact, he would. It turns out Smith is an *Ain't It Cool* fan—he'd met Harry in San Diego and, as Smith put it to me later, "We were able to geek mind-meld." Harcourt Fenton Knowles gave the green light. Schedules were juggled. Finally, last April, Mr. Smith and I talked on the phone.

For over two hours.

Talk about redlining your geek-o-meter. In this room, it pretty much goes without saying that Mr. Smith is widely considered one of the world's best living comic-book creators. For the last twelve years—working with his wife Vijaya and a single employee (the incredibly helpful and cool Kathleen)—Smith has self-published *Bone*, his fantasy saga about three creatures who look like the Brundle-chamber offspring of Pogo and the Shmoo. Bringing his animation background to the Bristol board, Smith created one of the most fluid, exciting all-ages comic books since Carl Barks was hammering away at *Uncle Scrooge*.

Along the way, Smith has collaborated on two *Bone* spinoffs—*Rose* (with Charles Vess) and *Stupid, Stupid Rat Tails* (with Tom Sniegoski)—and tried (and failed) to negotiate a *Bone* movie deal with Nickelodeon. And as his main series went on, it took on a surprising, *Lord of the Rings*-before-it-was-cool-again *gravitas*—focusing on the heroic journey of its human protagonist, Thorn, as she discovered her mystical "Dreaming" powers and royal past.

The story's going to end soon. Smith conceived of *Bone* as one long, self-contained tale. *Bone #55* will be the final issue; *Bone #51* hit the stands not too terribly long ago.

Over 120-odd minutes (and some follow-up e-mails), we talked about the final issues; Smith's upcoming work on *Captain Marvel*; exactly why the movie deal went to poo; Charles M. Schulz in a tux; the boxing-match feud with *Cerebus* creator Dave Sim; *Bone's* brief association with Image; Frank Miller; living up to "The Two Towers"; his background; self-publishing; his apparently quite awesome wife; and much, much, much, much more. An edited but still entirely too long transcript follows.

THE "LORD OF THE RINGS" INFLUENCE—AND *BONE'S* ORIGINAL, ANARCHIST STORYLINE

Alexandra DuPont: Now, you've said repeatedly that you've written the final pages of the "Bone" saga—you know how it's going to end.
Jeff Smith: Yeah.

DuPont: Now, what has it been—twelve years now?—and you're finally drawing those final pages. How much are you revising that script you wrote a decade ago?
Smith: In the broad outlines, it's very close. It's the same ending I've been steering toward. In the details, however, it's *completely* different.

I always knew that there would be some sort of confrontation at the end between the forces of the Locust and sister Briar versus Grandma and the Bones and the dragons. But the *actual* confrontation is nothing like I thought it was. And some of the personal conflicts between the actual characters I didn't foresee. But that's fun. I'm having a great time.

DuPont: Are there whole scenes that are being added to fulfill some of the character arcs that you've developed along the way?
Smith: Oh, absolutely. That's kind of happened the whole time. I mean, in the early days, I didn't plan on having the "Great Cow Race"—which became the story in comics that I'm most well-known for. That was not in my original outline—I just wanted to have Phoney Bone do something to get himself in trouble and fleece the local people out of their money, and it just became the cow race. And that's how it's gone for the past ten years: The characters have fallen into different troubles, and I just kind of go with them, and as soon as I see where it's going, I'll plot it out.

I did not see this big, climactic, fantasy battle at the end.

DuPont: Really?

Smith: I did not. In fact, I *fought* that—I did not want the big, Tolkien-esque, every-fantasy-story-has-it, free-for-all battle between the forces of good and evil. I just did not want it, I fought it—and it was just inevitable. [*laughs*]

DuPont: You're drawing this, and these fantastic *Lord of the Rings* movies have been coming out . . .

Smith: Yeah; I'm pretty thrilled with those.

DuPont: . . . and I was wondering if you were thinking, "Oh, poop! This is the stuff I was going to put on my pages, and now it's up on the screen!" Because there *are* some similarities in tone.

Smith: Yeah—and it's not really a coincidence. *Lord of the Rings* was really my model for the overall story structure. I definitely followed what I felt like was the *Lord of the Rings* path: I wanted to start with the Bones where you didn't feel like was a big, epic adventure—something I always hated in most fantasy: It always starts off with, "We're on an epic quest! And we're going to take five people and. . . ."

DuPont: Right. Your story didn't start out with, "AND BONE CAME DOWN FROM THE MOUNTAIN OF DOOM. . . . ."

Smith: Yeah. There was no prophecy that said that the little man would come and save them.

But I *did* end up having to have this big fantasy battle; it just was inevitable in the genre. I had gotten all the characters [to Atheia], and the good characters were inside the wall, and the bad characters were outside the wall surrounding them, and the battle began. And I had done all of my research; I had the correct medieval armor and weaponry. . . . I've read so many books on the sieges of medieval fortresses that you wouldn't believe it. And I actually drew *Bone #50* before the last *Lord of the Rings* film came out.

DuPont: Before Helm's Deep was put onscreen.

Smith: Before I saw that imagery the way Peter Jackson had put it together. And if you look at *Bone 50*, it's pretty paltry compared to what you see in *Lord of the Rings*. [*laughs*] And when I saw *The Two Towers,* I said, "Oh, my God—that guy just showed the *whole world* what this battle looks like, and now I have to go back!"

So in *Bone 51*, the battle scenes are on a much different scale; they're much more epic in scope—you know, I have more war ladders being put up. I mean, I had to—*Lord of the Rings* showed everybody what it can be. And when I collect *Bone* #50 into a book, I'm going to have to add some more soldiers. [*laughs*]

DuPont: So there will be kind of a "Special Edition" for the collected novel.
Smith: Oh, I always go back and completely redo the stories when I collect them in books. I re-edit them, even. For the last book, *Treasure Hunters*, I actually took some scenes from later comic books and moved them up earlier in the collected version, because a book has a different cadence to it than reading twenty pages every two or three months.

DuPont: Do you re-draw it, or do you use Photoshop so you can preserve your original art?
Smith: No, I get out the old art boards and I re-draw right on there. I add whole new pages. Add a lot of backgrounds.

Okay, so here's what I *originally* wanted to do [with the ending]: I wanted to tell a story where there was no government. I wanted the Bones and Grandma and all the characters of the valley to not need a government or a king or something like that—they could take care of themselves. And I had originally thought there might be characters who would come into the valley and try to impose bureaucracy on them. In fact, in the comic strip I did in college that *is* kind of the direction I went with it.

But when I was doing the comic book, it suddenly became apparent to me that the story I was telling was that Grandma Ben was going to march her granddaughter Thorn down south and put her back on the throne. And I was horrified by that idea. [*laughs*] I'm very anti-war, and I don't like really violent movies, and I was against the idea of having this big battle.

I remember talking to Vijaya and talking to some of my cartoonist buddies, and being dismayed that this was the direction that the story was going. And I was in a bar one night with Larry Marder—the cartoonist that does *Beanworld* and who now works for Todd McFarlane—and he heard my story, and he just looked at me and said, "Trust your story."

And from that point on, I was helpless: We were fighting to *preserve* the kingdom [*laughs*]—all the fantasy conventions fell into place, and I'm finding now that it's a better story.

DuPont: Well, you know, conventions are valuable. Conventions *work*, usually. It's the *riffing* on conventions that's interesting.
Smith: That's exactly right. What you have to do is avoid cliché.

For example, when it came time to depict the ancient city of Atheia, I wanted to stay away from the obvious European/King Arthur stereotype of most fantasy kingdoms. I needed an old place that was full of mysticism, that once had great glory, but has since fallen on hard times—and I decided to model Atheia on Kathmandu. Vijaya and I spent a week in Nepal. I walked around and took pictures and drew what it looks like—the narrow streets, the gutter where the houses meet the street, what kind of masonry they use. And I took pictures of alleys and temples, things that people have in their front yards. And all that's in the book. People who've been to Kathmandu have written me and said, "Oh—you got the prayer flags in the background, prayer stones, and all that stuff." That all comes from Nepal.

But what [modeling Atheia on Kathmandu] does is it breaks the cliché. It allows me to play and keep the convention fresh.

DuPont: You know, for someone who doesn't like violence, you just published one of the more disturbing comics sequences I've seen—where Briar reveals her face and it's Tarsil's before he was burned and then she slices Tarsil in half with a scythe.

Smith: Yeah. Dismemberment seems to be a running theme in my book. I think I should probably get myself checked out. [*laughs*]

DuPont: You're like Lucas with the limbs getting chopped off everywhere.

Smith: Yes, yes, yes. It's an image that occurs again and again in old stories. Couldn't tell you what it means, though. Life is violent, I guess.

FINAL-ISSUE HINTS (PLUS AN INVASIVE QUESTION ABOUT READERSHIP LOSS)

DuPont: Are you feeling an undue amount of pressure as you wrap these books up? Are you actually having more trouble producing these final four issues?

Smith: Um, yes I am. Part of it's just because there's a lot of battle scenes, and they really take a long time to draw. Also, I'm doing a lot of research. The first two-thirds of *Bone* took place in a fairy-tale forest—something I'm very familiar with and can make up. But [the final issues] take a *lot* of research.

I was talking to Frank Miller about these final battle scenes, and he said, "Well, what kind of military movement is that?" [I said,] "Oh, uh, I think it's a pincer movement." And he goes, "Mm-hmm. Yes it is. Okay." [*laughs*] I had to make real military movements; it had to feel very real.

DuPont: You have to vet things past the fellow who did 300.

Smith: Yes. [*laughs*] And there is pressure that I'm putting on myself to make sure that it pays off after twelve years. I want to make sure it's good. So I'm not skimping.

I have to say that the comic-book community has been extremely patient with me—especially in these last two or three issues, because they're running slow. But I'm definitely feeling support. Because they could be telling me to go take a long walk off a short pier, but they're not.

DuPont: Well, when you took a year off to go put together a *Bone* movie that was a risky thing to do. I mean, people who self-publish talk again and again about the fact that you really have to deliver something consistently if you're going to maintain your audience—because they *are* unforgiving. And you've tested audience patience a couple of times.

Smith: [*laughs*] Whatever do you mean?

DuPont: Have you paid a price on that level, readership-wise?

Smith: I've always been very worried about it. I took a very big chance when I put the book on hiatus to go work on the film. My gamble was, "If I come back with this good film, all will be forgiven!"

And of course the movie deal was becoming sour, to say the least, and I really began to panic—because I had no idea what I would come back to when I tried to start the book back up.

DuPont: Having Frank Miller and Alex Ross do alternate covers for your "comeback issue" [Issue #38] probably helps.

Smith: Yeah, having friends like Alex Ross and Frank Miller did help—and they did step in just for that very reason: to make sure that the first book I did on the way back would get everybody's attention.

And my numbers didn't seem to fail at all; in fact, obviously, the Frank Miller/Alex Ross issue sold very well, and then immediately my numbers were pretty much back where they were before—and have stayed there ever since then. I *apparently* have not paid much of a penalty, knock on wood.

DuPont: Right. Well, let's talk a little about issue 55, the final issue of *Bone*. You told the *A. V. Club*, and I quote, "There's some good fun/wow stuff coming." Care to offer any hints on what we'll be seeing?

Smith: Well. . . . One of the reasons I was able to accept a conventional good-versus-evil battle scene is because that is *not* how the book ends. I *do* have this other ending that involves Thorn and Fone Bone in the Dreaming with the Locust—and it's a very Stanley Kubrick thing. [*laughs*] And it's what I've been going for the whole time. It's a nice piece, and I can't wait to draw it. It's going to be hard, and it's a show-stopper in some ways.

Whether anybody *likes* it—that I can't promise. But that's about as much of a hint of that as I want to give.

DuPont: Now, we've seen images of a giant locust that represents the Lord of the Locust throughout the *Bone* books, including *Rose.* Is that what the Locust will *actually* look like when we really see him in the Dreaming with Thorn and Fone Bone?
Smith: We . . . will see him in action.

DuPont: Okay. Are there any panels in *Bone* #55 that you're dreading drawing?
Smith: Yes. There are some that are just technically going to be very difficult—little sequences—and there's some that are just going to be hard to draw because there's so much going on. I thought about getting some of my computer-animation friends to help me with some of these sequences—[have them make] models or something that I can trace, because there's going to be some crazy stuff to do.

DuPont: The first comic with animatics.
Smith: [*laughs*] Exactly! The first comic with Pre-Viz!

DuPont: I've read that Dave Sim and Gerhard, when they're drawing large structures, will actually build models of some of the buildings.
Smith: I've seen that. That's actually pretty cool. There's a lot to be said for staging—actually knowing where your characters are in relationship to the building they're in. It's very easy to confuse your readers if you don't give them visual clues to where everybody is in the room at all times.

I should point out that most of that ["fun/wow stuff"] is going to happen in issue fifty-four. Fifty-five will be the dessert. There's a lot of good stuff in fifty-five, but the real "fun/wow" stuff, that's gonna be fifty-four.

Oh, we're close. Things are falling apart right now. Wait 'til you go read fifty-two.

DuPont: Will we finally find out what young Thorn has been looking at when she's with all those dragons in the flashback sequences?
Smith: Oh, of course.

DuPont: Is it the Crown of Horns?
Smith: We'll have to see.

ORIGINS: *POGO*, JUVENILIA AND ANIMATION

DuPont: You've said that your early Ohio State *Lantern* college strips were sort of a cross between the current *Bone* and *Doonesbury*—but you've also said you don't like looking at those strips now. I'm just wondering why.
Smith: Well . . . because they suck. [*laughs*]

DuPont: Well. There you go.
Smith: They're just awful. I mean, *any* artist who looks back at something he did more than ten years ago is gonna cringe, just because the more you draw, the better you get—it's sort of automatic. And I look back at those, and they're so awful. I mean, the characters look different in every single panel, and the humor was all very sophomoric.

DuPont: So it was a typical college comic strip.
Smith: Any chance where I could have a tree limb tear Thorn's shirt off, that's what I needed to do, you know? [*laughs*]

DuPont: Has anyone ever turned up at a signing with one of those two thousand copies you sold of your college-strip collection?
Smith: About once a year, someone brings one up to me. And it's in crazy places—like in Finland. I guess they got it over eBay or something. . . . I have a box of about a hundred [books] left.

DuPont: The way you've described it, it sounds like you might have been striving for a bit of a *Pogo* tone in some of those early college strips.
Smith: Well, *Pogo* was a *huge* influence on me. I think I was nine when I saw a *Pogo* book; it was like 1969, and someone brought a *Pogo* collection book to school—a collection of the daily comic strips. And I was blown away by it—because not only was the artwork so gorgeous, and the line work was lush, but it looked like a Disney movie; that was the kind of quality that was in the cartooning.

And it was *fat;* a comic book that thick, I thought, was the greatest thing I'd ever seen. So I really studied Walt Kelly and *Pogo* from then on out.

DuPont: Didn't Walt Kelly work in animation? He used to *be* a Disney guy, didn't he?

Smith: Oh, yeah—he worked on *Pinocchio* and *Dumbo*. He worked on the famous crow sequence in *Dumbo*. He was a Disney animator, and after his Disney experience he came back to the East Coast and started doing *Pogo*.

DuPont: You have an animation background. How much animation training did you actually have?

Smith: Um, none. [*laughs*] A very good friend of mine from elementary school, we were in college together, and we were fascinated by animation. We shared a similar taste in comics and cartoons. We got a hold of a book that two Disney animators had done—Frank Thomas and Ollie Johnson—called *Disney Animation: The Illusion of Life*. And in it, two of Disney's Nine Old Men decided that they wanted to capture how they did the animation before it was too late—before it was gone.

We got this book and it was like, "Here's all the secrets to Disney animation"—and for fun, we would try them. We built our own little peg-boards and light-boxes, punched our own paper for registration holes, and taught ourselves out of that book. I can't remember when it came out, but it was the really early eighties, and Disney animation was pretty much a thing of the past. This was before *Little Mermaid*. . . . I think the best thing from that period was *The Aristocats*.

DuPont: So what kind of gigs was Character Builders, your animation company, doing?

Smith: Well, when we started, it was this friend I was talking about, Jim Kammerud, and another friend we'd met at Ohio State University, Marty Fuller. The three of us thought, "What if we could make some money doing local commercials?" And Marty had some contacts in the advertising industry, so we did a lot of public-service announcements and ads for local grocery stores.

And then, slowly, we began to get work from Hollywood studios that would have a big movie going on, and they would farm out individual scenes. We'd also work on television shows like *Doug;* they'd send us the storyboards and we would do all the layouts.

DuPont: So you're kind of a Disney alum by association.

Smith: I suppose, yeah. I don't think *Doug* was Disney back then. We worked on *Bébé's Kids* and *Rover Dangerfield*. [*pause*] We were not *responsible* for those.
. . .

And then, after I left Character Builders, I sold my share to my partners; they've gone on and worked on every animated feature film *except* for Disney that happened in the eighties and nineties—that huge boom. Now they do a lot of Disney direct-to-video sequels, like *Little Mermaid II* and the *101 Dalmatians* sequel, that kind of thing. They actually direct them and write them, in some cases.

DuPont: When you get the *Bone* series done, have you thought about going back to Character Builders?
Smith: Oh, well, that's who I went to Nickelodeon with [on the attempted *Bone* movie]. We gave that a shot—and maybe we'll do it again. Who knows?

SPEAKING OF WHICH: WHAT REALLY HAPPENED WITH NICKELODEON AND THE *BONE* MOVIE

DuPont: These days, comics have a lot more reverence for their characters on the big screen; recent Marvel films have been really strong, valuing character over effects. Does that bode well for you?
Smith: As far as doing a *Bone* movie? It might. It might. I think, when you talk about Hollywood, it ultimately comes down to [whether] the person with the money looks at the project and he or she thinks they're going to make their money back. As much as *Lord of the Rings* does sweeten the environment for me, it'll come down to that money person making a decision.

DuPont: Did you ever run into any trouble because the name of your property was *Bone?*
Smith: [*laughs*] Not in the way that you would think. No, not at all. In the mid-nineties, *Disney Adventures Digest,* that little check-out magazine, serialized *Bone* for about two years—it was very popular, but it also gave me the Good Housekeeping Seal of approval, you know? If *Disney* could run something called *Bone,* then that wasn't the problem.

DuPont: [*laughs*] Good point.
Smith: Where I ran into a problem is when we began having meetings about *Bone* with Nickelodeon, and we just began to overanalyze everything. They felt Thorn was the character who actually had the greatest story arc—which is true—and they're starting to think, "Well, maybe the movie should be called

'Thorn.'" And of course *Thorn* is what I called the strip in college, so I had this *opposite* realization and journey, where I took the story back to the Bones. But that's about the only time the name ever gave me trouble.

DuPont: Any truth to the reports that Nickelodeon wanted you to aim the story more squarely at kids?

Smith: Yes. Of course. I guess in some ways that's to be expected. But the truth is, we—meaning myself and the Character Builders and Vijaya—pitched Nickelodeon a fairly complete story idea. You know, we had big art boards made up, big beat boards, and we pretty much showed them the movie that we wanted to make—which would have been: The Bones get into the valley; they meet the princess; they're in the cow race; and they defeat the rat creatures. Very simple, straightforward movie.

DuPont: It would have set up a sequel if necessary.

Smith: Yeah. We had an ending in and of itself, but we could have gone on to finish the larger story in a sequel if it was warranted.

Well, we got into the meetings—and like immediately, they just wanted to change everything. They wanted the Bones to be voiced by six-year-olds—by children. They wanted to change the ending. They wanted the mood and tone of the story to be much more kid-friendly. And, I mean, we had talked about all this beforehand, so I was a little surprised.

For me, the famous moment was the suggestion that Fone Bone could have "magic gloves" so he could make things grow.

DuPont: Are those the green gloves that the Fone Bone figurine packaged with the color issue #1 is wearing?

Smith: Yes. Those are the magic gloves. He has one scene in the comic when he was wearing gloves because he was helping Thorn garden—and that just happened to be a picture that some of the licensees had picked up on and used a lot. So that became kind of the iconic drawing of Fone Bone, where he had these little gloves on.

Anyway. They said, "He should have magic gloves on so he can make things grow!" And I said, "He's not *Jesus Christ!* Come on!" [*laughs*]

DuPont: Oh, that's painful.

Smith: So it was a bit like negotiating through a swamp.

DuPont: Any truth that they wanted a Britney Spears-style pop song?

Smith: No, they didn't want a Britney Spears-style pop song—they wanted a *Britney Spears* song in the film. And I like Britney Spears; I like pop culture; I like Madonna and Michael Jackson as much as anybody else—but I had a very different kind of a film that I was trying to make.

And in the late nineties, I was really adamant that there would be no songs in the movie—because all animated feature films seem to have these awful formulaic songs. I think that's a law somewhere—"Animated film for kids? Put some crappy songs in it!"

Like when we pitched Warner Bros. while we were in Annecy. They took us out on a boat and were really wooing us—until I got to the point where I said, "I need it in writing that there will be no songs." And it was pretty much, "Swim back to shore." [*laughs*] That was it. That was the end.

But Nickelodeon did agree to no songs. In writing. So this pop-song thing was probably the turning point in the whole affair for me; this was about a year-and-a-half in. I mean, we had a great *time* with Nickelodeon—they were a lot of fun, the actual executives that we worked with. I really liked them. We would go to New York, where Viacom is, or we would go to Paramount, and we always had a wonderful time. But one day after lunch we sat down . . . and the executive there turned to me and said, "Okay. We can get twelve million dollars right now if we put a pop song in the movie. So, *Jeff*—do you see somewhere in the body of the film where we could put a Britney Spears or an NSYNC song?"

DuPont: Oh my God.

Smith: And I just turned and looked at Vijaya, we looked at each other, and I said, "No." I mean, that's not the kind of movie that we were making. I mean, you wouldn't put a Britney Spears song in the middle of *The Empire Strikes Back* or the middle of *Lord of the Rings*. And because Vijaya had insisted that clause be in the contract, they couldn't force me.

Things went downhill rapidly after that. I think I became, instead of "the director and the writer," I suddenly became "the creator who was being too protective of his little baby."

DuPont: "The person they had to wrest it from."

Smith: Yes, yes. I was being too sensitive.

DuPont: Did you ever have a moment where they said, "You're being too sensitive, Jeff"?

Smith: Oh, of course. [*laughs*] They were trying to be very gentle with me because I was the creator and I didn't want to see my babies hurt. They didn't see me as a filmmaker with a vision—at least not after I turned down twelve million dollars. [*laughs*]

DuPont: So basically, it ate up your time, it bore little fruit, it was frustrating. Did this further validate your decision to self-publish?
Smith: Well, let me go back and say that I didn't think it was *that* frustrating, and I didn't think it was a waste of time. I enjoyed the experience quite a bit, and it was not *all* Nickelodeon's fault; part of it was my own inexperience in the system. If I could go back in time and do it again, I would have sat down first thing and storyboarded the movie that we had all agreed on to begin with. I didn't know to do that then. I didn't know—I kept thinking there would be a moment where someone would say, "Okay—start now." Do you know what I mean? So I actually thought it was a pretty good experience. I got to learn a lot about Hollywood; I got to learn a lot about story structure. In Nickelodeon's defense, they found weak points in my story—and they held my feet to the fire until I screamed and figured them out. And they ultimately did agree to a contract that allowed me to keep my rights when it didn't work out. That isn't the *juicy* part of the story to tell, but that's the truth.

And also, everything I do affects my comics. So not one bit of that was wasted time. I mean, it was a *gamble*—I could have lost my readership in comics—but that didn't happen. What was the other part of your question?

DuPont: Did this further validate your decision to self-publish?
Smith: In a way, yeah. I mean, it has been our experience—Vijaya's and mine—that *Bone* only works when we do it ourselves. The syndicates were interested in *Bone* as a comic strip, but ultimately they couldn't sell it the way we wanted to do it—and the same with Nickelodeon.

DuPont: What are the chances that you'll revisit the film deal after you're done making the books?
Smith: Well, I'd like to, to be honest. But will I *get* to? I don't know. It might be one of those things you just get the one shot at, so who knows?

But my plan is when the comic book is done, and while I'm finishing up *Captain Marvel,* I plan on putting together another script. And I got a lot of calls from other studios and producers once I *left* Nickelodeon, and I tried to be polite and say, "Well, you know, I'd like to finish the book; can I call you back later?" So we'll see. I have a lot of phone numbers. . . . Maybe the time will have come and gone. We'll see.

DuPont: So if I'm hearing you correctly, next time you're going to basically do what Peter Jackson did with *Lord of the Rings*—he basically had the whole movie storyboarded in advance. He showed the cast the whole film in storyboards with temp-track voices.

Smith: That's exactly right. And my understanding is that quite a few directors do that—Miyazaki, for instance—not just Peter Jackson. I mean, they see the movie in their head.

A Conversation with Jeff Smith

LUCY SHELTON CASWELL AND DAVID FILIPI / 2007

Jeff Smith: Bone and Beyond. Ed. Lucy Shelton Caswell and David Filipi. Columbus: Wexner Center for the Arts, 2008. Reprinted with permission.

David Filipi: Can you remember when you were first exposed to the work of some of the people you have cited as influences, who are included in the show?

Jeff Smith: *Peanuts* was almost unavoidable. Everybody read *Peanuts*, especially in the 1960s, because it was in the Sunday paper. But I actually remember the first time *Peanuts* got under my skin was when my mom bought me a little paperback collection, like one of those little twenty-five-cent paperbacks. It was mostly silent. It was a collection of Snoopy strips. There wasn't a lot of talking so I could almost read it. This would have been when I was about four—so before I was even able to read.

And I remember that what actually got me to learn to read was trying to figure out what was happening with Snoopy and Charlie Brown in these little book collections, because I didn't have my parents there reading to me like I did with the Sunday paper. I was by myself with this book, and I just had to figure out what Charlie Brown and Snoopy were doing.

Filipi: It is interesting that you mentioned Charles Schulz first because one can assume that you would be exposed to Charlie Brown and *Peanuts* at an early age. But how does someone your age get exposed to E. C. Segar, George Herriman, and people like that? It is unlikely you would just walk into a store and find reprints.

Smith: Some of the influences are the kind that you see at a very early age and some come almost by osmosis—they get into you. It's not like I studied Schulz. He informed my sense of humor in the way I drew faces and things like that. Then there are the influences that you get later on. When I was going to Ohio State, I met Lucy and she had the early incarnation of the Cartoon

Research Library. That was the first time I saw some real serious collections of old, classic, golden age newspaper strips. In the library, I found a book of the old Segar *Thimble Theatres* that reprinted the first year of the strip, and it blew me away. At that time, I was already doing *Thorn*, which was basically an early version of *Bone*, in the Ohio State *Lantern*, but it was still unformed, a beginning version. Segar changed the texture of the strip: I picked up his more abrupt sense of humor and pacing, and that began to work its way into the *Thorn* strip from that point on.

Filipi: When you say the "abrupt" pacing, what do you mean?
Smith: His jokes were kind of coarse—and fast. When you make a comic you always have to be aware of any two given panels working together. What happens to the subject from one panel to the next defines the amount of time that takes place between the two panels. So, in a Segar comic, if Popeye's in jail, when he wants to get out of jail, he just tears the bars down. Segar wouldn't waste any panels of *Popeye* pulling on the bars. One second he's standing there; the next second the bars are flying. That's what I meant by abruptness. He intuitively knew how to pace the drawings in the panels. I call it "abrupt" because it catches you off guard—it's a bit of surprise—and it's a large part of his sense of humor. I started using that in the strips a lot, too. I discovered Herriman around the same time, probably in comic book stores. In comic book stores, I began to see a more layered world of comics, where you had the undergrounds, you had alternatives, you had *Superman*, and you had collections being put out by, say, Kitchen Sink, of *Krazy Kat*. And they were really beautiful reproductions. There's real care being put into these books. And there's another kind of . . . I won't use the same word, it's not abrupt . . . but there's an edginess to Herriman's work, a looseness. Instead of saying "abrupt," I'll say it's more immediate. It feels like there's a stage of refinement missing in between Herriman and the reader that just feels more immediate.

Lucy Shelton Caswell: I want to go back to *Peanuts* and ask what was it that grabbed you about that comic strip?
Smith: The fact that the characters were thinking. Portraying the interior lives of these kids was so unprecedented at the time. I probably didn't think in those terms when I was five or six, but I still knew it, because you could watch cartoons on TV, you could see Bugs Bunny, you could see Heckle and Jeckle—these are all really good cartoons, but nobody talked about the troubling interior life the way Schulz did, and did so perfectly. When Charlie Brown made a fool of himself, or was embarrassed by the other kids, or he

said his stomach hurt, you could see on his face that his stomach hurt. With two dots, and a squiggly line for a mouth, he showed you what Charlie Brown felt, and that is remarkable. He has such a wide range of characters—from Snoopy to Lucy and Linus and Schroeder—he just covered such a wide range of human emotion. Again, I didn't think about that when I was a kid—probably nobody really does—but it reaches you. And so that's why I think it works so well.

Filipi: You mentioned that early on you were more influenced by strips or perhaps "influenced" is not the right word at that time in your life, but you were more exposed to comic strips than to comic books. It's interesting that a lot of your influences in the show are strip artists, yet *Bone* is not a strip work. It's a longer-form work. How did that happen? Why were you not more influenced by longer-form artists?
Smith: Well, the short answer is that there weren't too many longer-form artists back then.

Filipi: I meant working with an issue of a comic book as opposed to a strip.
Smith: I think it's because the two art forms have such different working methods. The comic strip started off as sort of an auteur medium where you had a single artist who wrote it and drew the strip. The comic books from the beginning were a very commercial enterprise where you had an editor or a company that was creating characters for sale, and they would hire someone to write it and hire somebody else to pencil it. It was a real factory process creating that kind of a book. They had somebody doing the lettering, somebody doing the inking. There was some of that in comic strips, but not to the same extent. I was just more drawn to the auteur work. That's why when I found the comic book stores, and I discovered the auteur work in the independent comic books, that's when I began a shift toward them. Also, I submitted my comic strip to every syndicate that existed, and they all turned me down. So, I didn't have any choice.

Caswell: You did have a choice. You could have done it and adapted it the way some of them suggested.
Smith: That's very true. And that's why when I discovered a place that I felt was a more fertile ground for my type of comics—comic books—I didn't hesitate to move over in that direction. So, I actually don't see that much of a disconnect between the kind of influences that we're including in the show like Herriman and Schulz and comic books, because it's that single-author-ness

that is the connection between those strips and my work. And there are certainly other comic book artists that fit that category now.

Caswell: You came to know what your direction was as a very young person. I think that's rather unusual.
Smith: It sounds more unusual than it seems, I think, because even though I loved comics and I wanted to do them, I didn't set out to be a cartoonist or anything like that from the get-go. I didn't say, "I know what I'm going to do and I'm going to do it: like Mozart writing symphonies and never looking back. I went through high school, and I did not know what I was going to do for a living. I had no idea. I didn't know if I was going to get into animation and go and try and get a job at Disney. The fact that I ended up, once I got into college, actually really trying to do what I wanted to do as a little kid, kind of brought the circle back around. I'm not trying to say I knew I was going to be a cartoonist the whole way through.

Caswell: You did a sort of prototype of the story that became *Bone* as an undergraduate and had the arc of story already percolating in your mind.
Smith: Right. Interestingly, I didn't. When I started the comic strip in college, I was very jazzed by certain strips, like *Doonesbury*, which had a lightly continuing storyline that would go on for very long periods, and of course *my* childhood loves of *Peanuts* and *Uncle Scrooge*. Then the last big, big influence on me before I started the comic was *Métal Hurlant*, *Heavy Metal*, Moebius and Enki Bilal, and all those guys doing kind of grownup fantasy stories or mythological stories. So being able to mix those kinds of things together— *Doonesbury* and *Uncle Scrooge* and *Heavy Metal*—that was what I felt was the subject matter that would interest me, and I came up with the cast while drawing the comic strip. But it actually bugged me that I didn't have a story. I had these three Bone characters, and they all had personalities, and it seemed like there was a lot I could do with them. They were really fun to work with. And I had all these characters for them to work against—the dragons and the monsters and the humans that lived in the environment. But there was no point to it, and it kind of bugged me. Why don't these characters have some reason for being in this story? I started to understand that I was missing an underpinning. I was missing some depth. I wanted to find out what inspired George Lucas and what inspired Tolkien. And that's how I discovered Joseph Campbell, who was a big inspiration for Lucas to build his *Star Wars* stories on mythology. So, from Lucas and Joseph Campbell, I started reading mythology starting with Greek mythology, but then discovering Indian mythologies. It

was the same with Tolkien. Tolkien was all Celtic folktales and stuff, and I really got into that material. I began to understand that there are two directions for a story. There is the linear one that goes from beginning to middle and end, which I always wanted to do from the time I was a kid. But what builds that story? That's where you get into the symbolism and mythology . . . that's the art. And that gives it depth.

Filipi: So, you were consciously combining the art stories and the mythological works that you were reading at the same time? You were very conscious of that?

Smith: I was very conscious of it. My thought was if you're going to put this much work into something—because comics are a heck of a lot of work—it better be something you like to draw. And the two things that interested me were the *Heavy Metal* adult-fantasy type of comics, and *Pogo* and the Carl Barks's *Uncle Scrooge* material. I just thought you can put those two together, and I thought you would have something that would meld and be funny and entertaining. That's what I wanted to work in. And it wasn't until later that it began to feel that it needed more, that it needed a depth to it that I found in symbolism and mythology.

Filipi: I think part of it, too, is getting older and getting more life experience.

Smith: Certainly. By the time I finished *Bone*, which was a thirteen-year process, I had begun to travel. As *Bone* got published in more and more languages, Vijaya and I were being invited to different countries. We would explore all of the cathedrals and the art we would see there, the culture there. Then my life experiences began to really impact *Bone*, which worked because the Bones were having the same experience in the story as they explored the valley and found new civilizations. So, yes, it does. I guess as you get older you are more interested in symbolism in art anyway.

Filipi: It sounds like a natural progression where you created the characters and you created the world that you wanted them to inhabit, but you were frustrated because you wanted there to be more meaning in what you were working on. It seems natural to me that after being exposed to all different types of things in college that you would want to expand it.

Smith: I thought because *Bone* was a serialized story that took years to complete, I would get feedback and I would find that people would enjoy things that had some meat to them. People enjoy things that have meaning. It became one of the secret pleasures of making comics—doing this research, blocking out time in my work day to go online and just follow one myth through its many permutations around the world, or to plan a trip to Kathmandu and go spend time and say, "This is going to be an alleyway right here that is going to appear in *Bone*." I started to really, really enjoy doing the research—and then always felt like there was a lot of reward for doing it because I could tell people would be enthusiastic about the results.

Filipi: A minute ago you mentioned Carl Barks, and a number of people have noted the similarities between *Bone* and Barks's *Uncle Scrooge* stories. Do you remember the effect these stories had on you?

Smith: I remember there was nothing else like them. In those days, artists who worked on Disney comics were anonymous, but you could tell when Barks did a story. His art was so good. The line work on the characters was fine and detailed and the backgrounds were realistic. His stories were little gems. But it was the comics work itself that really grabbed me. His compositions and the positions of the characters within the frames as they transitioned from one panel to the next are kinetic. How far they had moved conveyed action, movement, and life. Those shirt-wearing ducks were real!

Caswell: Can you talk a little bit about Will Eisner?

Smith: Yes, I sure can. I first met him at Ohio State when he came to do a talk. I brought with me the first Will Eisner comic I encountered. And that's probably a better place to start. I found this reprint of his stuff. It was black and white—like an oversized magazine—in the early 1970s. So, I was still a kid. I was probably ten or eleven, and I just was really knocked out by his artwork. His line style was filled with those really graceful thicks and thins—the same kind of thing that appealed to me about Walt Kelly's line work. It was superb—extremely appealing. It was really dense and kind of dangerous at the same time. His stories were kind of superhero stories. The superhero guy had a suit on, but he still had a mask, which appealed to me as a kid. But the difference was that his stories had a *Twilight Zone* twist to them—an O'Henry type of twist. So, they had the feeling of a short story, which gave them that heft or that weight that I said I felt was missing from my early comics. And I think it's missing from ninety-nine percent of all comics. But he had that in there. He had stories that were doing something, that were going somewhere. His characters were fully realized. And his work continued to have that kind of quality all the way up until he died.

Of course, in our industry, the comics industry, the major awards are named after him. While he was still alive, he would actually stand on stage during the Eisner Awards. He wasn't the presenter, but he would actually shake your hand and hand you your Eisner Award, when you went upstage. That was very exciting when I won my first Eisner Award. I felt he was genuinely happy for me. I actually got to know him quite well and over the next ten years, which is how long he lived after I first met him, I would see him at different comic-book shows, and I'd try to get some time with him in a bar or for a meal or something. He was one of those inspirational people. His mind never stopped thinking about comics and where they could go and what they could do, and what was the best potential for the reader. He was the guy who popularized the term "graphic novel" and was the first one to do one worthy of the name. I could go on and on about Will. I mean, as a human being he was just warm and supportive, and he never missed an opportunity to pat you on the back and tell you to keep going.

Filipi: Did you ever talk with him specifically about how he rewrote some of the rules: the layout of a page, the disregard for borders and panels and things like that?

Smith: I personally never actually consciously approached page layouts the way that how-to books tell you. I never found any of them to be very helpful, including Will's. However, there were many other elements of Will's how-to books that do express some kinds of movement—and the fact that he was one of the first to do it just gave it some weight. The one page layout I did use of Will's was what he calls the "meta-panel," which is where you have a large panel with insets. Usually it is used to convey some importance to the larger image. But I never spoke to him about that at all. What we would talk about would usually be industry matters. When I knew Will, the comic book industry was going through a very hard time. It was crashing, losing sales, stores were going out of business. This potential to take the graphic novel into the outer market was looming, but could we make it? Could we make the jump? We didn't know if it would happen, and we would talk a lot about that.

Caswell: In many ways, you and Will both marched to a different drummer.

Smith: I think Will recognized me as a fellow traveler, that's for sure. When you're talking about art, you can't have those kinds of concerns. To do something that doesn't fit into anything could make it great art, but not necessarily. But it makes some sense to abide by some rules. Like trying to get your comic book to try to fit into a certain category so that people can sell it. Unlike a Matisse or a Picasso, these are popular art, mass art. You do want them to get out and get distributed. In that way comics have more in common with film than paintings. Because the original art is not the final product—the final product is the printed, mass-produced comic book. So, the original page of art is sort of like the set or the script for a movie. The final product, of course, is the film. So, what we're showing in this exhibit, I guess, would be like the equivalent of movie sets.

Caswell: Is there an anomaly then in doing gallery shows of original pages?
Smith: No, because there is an art in the comics. The art is kind of intangible, and the only people that really talked about it with any length or weight are Will Eisner and Scott McCloud. But there is an art to it. There is an art being communicated from the artist to the reader, and not in every comic, and not every idea is successful, but you have to approach it as art. That gets back to the breaking rules thing. Art just doesn't do well with rules. Art, in fact, thrives when the rules get broken. That's why people like me started trying to collect the books into these graphic novels to try to launch them out of our little tiny distribution system and get them into the other stores. I was part of a whole wave of artists that took up that call—just wouldn't do what we were supposed to do. But that's what is fun. That's what gets people interested. Now, many people are breaking the rules. More power to them. Break the rules, go on the Internet, and go forever. That was something Will Eisner would have said to me.

Filipi: Just from looking at *Bone* there are definitely Joe Kubert influences. Could you talk about him?
Smith: What struck me about Kubert's work—in both of his most famous titles, *Sgt. Rock* and *Tarzan*—was his artwork. He had a completely individual line, like nobody else's—a big, fat, kind of greasy ink line that broke and blotched. And he didn't obsess about details, and in fact he would often leave out information. He might not even draw somebody's feet, but you always knew where the feet were. I came to appreciate that his artwork was in some ways better than the people who were drawing really perfect anatomically correct people. He engaged your imagination. I definitely brought that into my *Bone* work. Nothing I draw looks like Joe Kubert, but I was very conscious of how much information you had to impart because Joe knew exactly how much he needed to sell the idea completely. And I actually think that's more powerful—when you, the reader, fill in the feet. You do more than fill in the feet when you're doing that. You're filling in everything around the feet and behind them, and you make the world all the more real. The storytelling was really powerful. He could make an adventure story move. One minute he could

have Tarzan standing there talking to someone, and you got Tarzan standing with his weight on one leg, like a real human would, instead of standing there with his hands on his hips like a superhero, and the next minute he's in the trees carrying a human being chased by gorillas, and it all looked completely real. It looked like that's really happening—and trees that are a hundred-stories tall. It's just how he can make something impossible feel so plausible that you could almost feel the sunlight splashing by him and feel tree limbs under your feet. It's just amazing to me. Do you know how disappointed I was when I found out that trees in Africa weren't as tall as the Empire State building?

Filipi: In a totally different vein, what about Garry Trudeau?
Smith: Well, Garry Trudeau stimulated my curiosity about politics and about the way politics work. When I say "politics" I don't just mean senators. I mean the way our media works. Kelly interested me in politics when I was younger, but Trudeau explained it. He showed the relationship of the media to the senators and to the lobbyists in a way that was funny and told you more than the actual news told you, because it was true.

It was satire, but there is satire in other media. There is satire on TV. I was reading all that stuff at the same time *All in the Family* was on. But, to this day I don't think you can find more truth in any other medium than in comics. I think that kind of artist—like a political cartoonist—blows away all the clouds of games and all that kind of stuff and just gets to the stripped-down truth of the matter. I've always felt that way, even as a kid, first with *Mad* magazine and then with *Pogo*. There was nowhere else you could look and gel that kind of truth about what was really going on. You sure couldn't get it from commercials or TV. Most sitcoms and commercials are unbearable to me. I never thought movies were false or anything, but I always felt that movies were really beautiful structured pieces of art that were stories—sort of like novels. Comics were where I was told the truth. That's the only place I could get the truth—*Mad* magazine and *Pogo* and *Doonesbury* and, really, *Peanuts*. That was real stuff. That was real interaction, there was no hiding. That is how the dirty stuff works. That's reality. Of course, Trudeau also developed his own comics pacing, with those four identical panels that he painstakingly redrew with just the smallest facial tic . . . and the penultimate panel. With those two innovations, he made it to the top pantheon as far as I'm concerned.

Caswell: A lot of people don't think about the writing part of comics. Can you talk about your influences in writing?

Smith: My biggest influences in writing comics is Walt Kelly. The ability to have dialogue come from different characters in *Pogo*, and have that dialogue grounded in that character's personality, is unrivaled. But also, a lot of my writing influences come from outside of comics. I really like a lot of movies, like *Casablanca*—like that complicated and yet very simple and perfectly formed puzzle that creates a story. I really like things that start off very simple and childlike, like *Huckleberry Finn* or even *The Odyssey*. I can't think of any other examples right now, but as the story goes on the themes become much more complex and adult and dark sometimes. That is the kind of story that I'm drawn to and that I want to try to tell.

When you asked that, I first thought of the kind of writing that doesn't involve words. In comics, you are writing with blocks of panel—blocks of art—that sometimes include word balloons. So, to me, as I mentioned earlier, the smallest basic unit of writing in comics is any two given panels, because those two panels play off each other—and then of course the next two panels. So, it is always just the two panels leaping over that gutter that creates the writing. What I was talking about with the pacing—making sure the reader's eye doesn't spend too much time on a panel when you don't want it to—all of that goes into writing in comics. The best way to explain this might be to share an example of a time I had a lot of readers mad at me when I did one comic: *Bone* #16.

I had a twenty-page comic to do, and I thought it would be fun to try an experiment and to present the comic in real time; that is to say the amount of time it would take the reader to open up the front cover, start reading the comic, and by the time he closes it—say it was fifteen minutes, twenty minutes, or whatever, however long it took them to read that comic—that's how much time it took for the characters inside the story to do whatever they had to do. Since the subject matter was the Bones being chased through a stormy forest, I had all sorts of opportunity to create atmosphere, to try to have suspense, because they didn't know where the monsters were in this dark, stormy forest—all around them or right next to them. They wouldn't know if they were nearby unless there was a lightning flash. So, I did an entire twenty-page comic like I just described. There are some words but not a lot. It takes fifteen minutes for them to run through this forest and evade all these monsters, and it takes fifteen minutes to read it. That was a lot of fun to do, and I had a lot of cartoonist friends write me or call me and say that they really dug it—they liked it a lot. . . . it was one of their favorite things. But the readers . . . oh my gosh, I got so much hate mail. I couldn't believe it. A lot of people thought I was ripping them off because they paid full price for this comic, but there were no words in it. I was really surprised by that. It was an eye-opening experience. Because it took me just as long to draw every panel, whether it had words or not.

Filipi: Did comics serve as an escape for you as a kid or a way of learning about the world around you?

Smith: I think I can honestly say it was both. I would love to get a comic book and then couldn't wait to go sit somewhere and read it. As soon as you start reading, the world's gone. But it was always a way to filter the world I was looking at. That probably comes from *Mad* magazine and *Pogo,* because *Pogo* was unashamedly a giant metaphor for human foibles and politics. So, it was always a way to talk about real life. And to me, that is the art part. That is what makes it art.

Filipi: You brought up the concept of the auteur in comic strips, the idea of one person drawing and writing the strip. How young were you when you were aware of that?

Smith: I think I must have been pretty young, five. I knew that Walt Disney was on TV every Sunday night back in the 1960s and you knew that he made up Mickey Mouse, right? And the same with Walter Lantz who made up Woody Woodpecker, and Charles Schulz with Snoopy. So, I think very early on I knew cartoons had cartoonists. Fone Bone was my early attempt to come up with a Snoopy or a Mickey Mouse or something. I was definitely aware of it very early on.

Filipi: Were you aware of the distinction between a single artist working on *Peanuts* and, say, a group of people working on a *Superman* comic book?

Smith: No, of course not.

Filipi: Not when you were five, but maybe when you were twelve or thirteen?

Smith: In the early days of comics they didn't credit the different artists that came together to make a book. But by the time I was eight or nine, it was starting to be a little more common practice. You knew that Jack Kirby was drawing *Fantastic Four*, and you knew that Neal Adams was drawing *Batman* and *Green Lantern.* By the time I was ten I was seeking out Neal Adams or Joe Kubert on a book. I was looking for that individual artist to follow his progression, because he got better every single issue—it was just so exciting.

Caswell: How do you decide what part of the story not to tell versus what you want to tell?

Smith: In some cases, you can make a dramatic decision that things "off-screen," so to speak, have more impact. A famous example is Bambi's mother getting killed. People think that is such a big dramatic, violent event, but it's actually never seen on screen. It takes place when the camera's following Bambi running away. I actually think that adds power and weight to it. I was trying to think of an example of me doing that. I know I did. There is violence in *Bone*, but I only occasionally show it. So sometimes you do that. Other times you make decisions on what is the most interesting. What is the most immediate thing happening. And you have to draw that because that is what engages.

Filipi: In *Bone* we never see Boneville. We only hear about why the Bones left Boneville.

Smith: That kind of falls into the dramatic thing, where you decide that something is going to have more weight if it's not seen. I started to get letters from people saying, "Oh I can't wait to see Boneville." And then they would describe what they thought Boneville looked like. Nobody's descriptions were the same. Some of them were really imaginative. I realized I just wasn't going to show Boneville then because I could tell that it had much more weight for each reader when they made it up themselves. That's one of the problems I've had with Hollywood when they want to start a screenplay. They always want to start in Boneville because it's a much more linear way to start a story. And I just can't. I can't let them. But I think your question really is not about those decisions. You're asking about what do you decide to draw, because if it's a continuum of motion or an action that is going on, what do you pick? And I don't know. I think about when I used to animate, and you learn to zero in on key moments that communicate the most.

Filipi: There are points in the story where two pages could be one drawing. How do you determine what needs to be fully drawn out and emphasized by showing greater detail?

Smith: Part of that comes down to process. At some point you move on instinct—like when I'm writing the scripts and I rough them out. As I start to build up the pages, first they're in pencil and then more and more ink, then the lettering goes on. . . . For each step, I read the panels over and over again, trying to stay with the rhythm that's being created. If you want it to go faster—if it is going too slow—and you feel like the story should hop a little more, you can do things to speed up what's going on. You can take some words out, or take away some detail. Sometimes as your eye moves through a panel, when it's in pencil, the timing looks great. When I ink it, some big solid block or a little piece of detail might catch your eye and slow you down, and you spend a little too much time on that panel—and linger—before you go to the next panel. So, in the process, you just have to continue to reread it and refine it and make sure that the speed is all there. Hopefully before you get that far along in the script stage, you'll have caught an extra beat that you don't need and you can get rid of that.

Caswell: Can you talk a little bit about the double-page spreads in which you then place smaller panels, the kind of layout Eisner called a "meta-panel"? How do you imagine readers approaching those pages?

Smith: Everything has to do with placement . I rarely do a doublepage spread. That's when you have the book flat open and the entire surface of the book is a single panel. Sometimes you can set a panel inside that panel. It depends where you put the panel. If you put the little inset panel—a little circle or a little square or whatever—in the upper left, then it is likely going to get looked at first. Because reading comics is identical to reading prose: you start in the upper left and go left to right, top to bottom, just like in any other book. You turn the page, and if there's a panel up there, you, as a Western reader, are automatically going to go up there. So, as an author, you have some choices to make. If you're going to use a double-page spread, you're going to make that choice because you want the impact of a panel that large. This is such a complicated topic.

There is a build-up to a splash page. I normally put about six panels to a page. A lot of people do eight panels to a page. But what you do is establish a rhythm of your six panels a page, and then if, suddenly, a whole page or two pages are used for a larger image, it is going to have an impact. So, you've made the decision to use this double-page spread . . . Sometimes you might want to set something inside it, sometimes not. It just depends on timing. If it is a big double-page spread of, say, the valley, and that image is timeless, then I may want to have a character speak without putting a balloon in that big, beautiful image. I may put a little panel down there and have the character say something—"Wow, what a great view!"—or maybe something more tied into the story. But that would then imply to me that he was saying that standing there looking out over that valley. The story's not moving on. I want him to be still standing there and for the reader to *feel* that view as he's saying it. Whereas if I wanted the story to move on, if they were confronted by an army or something, and that was the double-page spread conveying a massive size, I might not want to have a character stand there and say anything. I might want to turn the page, and then I wouldn't use a double-page spread or I wouldn't put any message in there. So it is a question of placement and timing. Do I want people to feel 1ike they're in this image? I never thought about that before. But that's actually totally what you're doing.

Filipi: When filmmakers are preparing for a film, they often will go back and watch other directors' films—or maybe tell their cinematographer or art director, "I want you to watch these films" for inspiration. Obviously, it's different because you're working by yourself. Maybe you didn't do that with *Bone,* but when you're working on projects now, do you look at other people's work to inform your own?

Smith: I rarely look at comics or comic books for that kind of influence. I *will* look at movies. That is where I go for inspiration on composition of a frame, or even a story structure. I've just been drawn to that kind of thing. That is why I've been always drawn more toward the longer form of comics, because it fits with my notion of story, which has more in common with film and books than with traditional comics, which have always been a very ephemeral art form. Charlie Brown never ages and he goes on and on and on and on. He never even changes his shirt. So just in the last twenty years, really, have comics begun to move into this new kind of storytelling, which is a little more like a novel or like a film—something with a beginning, and a middle, and an end—a structure like that, as opposed to just an open-ended soap opera . . . like Spiderman never kissing his girlfriend, or whatever.

Filipi: You mentioned how comics have changed over the last twenty years or so. One way that *Bone* really stands out from some of the other acclaimed graphic novels, recently anyway, is that so many of them are either autobiographical or they're about historical events in one way or another, whereas *Bone* is completely original, fictional, narrative. Why do you think so many people are turning to the graphic novel medium to tell their life stories?

Smith: That's a good question. I believe it's rooted in the past of comics, like the traditions that Robert Crumb started. The underground comics were a reaction to the corporate, cleaned-up comics that Robert Crumb was reading in the 1950s. Instead of these packaged comics done by factories, he wanted to do the opposite. He was trying to do real life—his thoughts, his pains—and everything the establishment didn't like, he wanted to put in there. So, there is a long tradition in underground comics of autobiographical material.

There are also the comics that read like literary fiction, that aren't necessarily autobiography but tales grounded in postmodern life. There are a lot of really good artists working in that genre right now, like Dan Clowes and Chris Ware. I think that if they weren't doing such strong work, there wouldn't be the interest in it. It is also easier for the critics to hold onto it. There's something about working in an office and being alienated in your cubicle . . . there is a lot more for a critic to hold onto than with fantasy stories with flying monsters and wizards and stuff.

Filipi: It's interesting to me how Marjane Satrapi's *Persepolis* books drew multiple articles in the *New York Times*. I think part of it was that they were able to treat it in a different way because it was about political issues and cultural issues. It's almost as if that gave the newspaper a greater license to put it on the front page of the arts section.

Smith: *Persepolis* has multiple hooks because not only is it autobiographical, but it's topical. It's a woman working in a medium where very few women are excelling, and it's about a woman who is writing about Iran, where women are repressed. So you have all kinds of hooks, and it's also really good. That's the kind of thing that hits. I kind of said that all backwards, because what I really meant is it's good, but it also has a hook by being about so many topical things.

Filipi: That is not just true for comic books, it is true for, say, film as well. It's kind of ridiculous to use the Academy Awards as an example, but you rarely see a comedy, for instance, winning all the awards. It's usually films about political subjects or other serious subjects.

Smith: *Bone* has been very unusual in that it's had that critical acclaim, and it doesn't fit the mold. I never quite understood what drew critics to it. It started being picked up critically at a time when comics were experiencing a real commercial crush: the collectors' market had taken over and comic publishers were manufacturing "chase" comics—super special comics that you had to order a hundred normal issues in order to get the one that had a fold-out cover. At that time *Bone* emerged as a hand-drawn book being done out of my garage, and at the same time the garage music scene was happening in Seattle. A lot of the critics grabbed on to *Bone* because it was high profile enough that it was something that they could say, "This works." I got lucky that it kind of popped out and got out of the fantasy/comedy rut that it could've gotten stuck in very easily.

Caswell: Why do you think critics don't take fiction more seriously in the graphic novel world?

Smith: I like to find that *Time* top ten list to see what is on there. Most of the choices are like *Blankets* and *Fun Home* . . . but *Bone*'s not the only fantasy one is it? *David Boring* and *Ed the Happy Clown*. That's crazy stuff. *Jimmy Corrigan, Palomar*. Alan Moore's *Watchmen*, that's superheroes. I'm wondering if it's not quite as bad as it seems. When the very first people go out on a limb to talk about comics in a big publication like *Time* or the *New York Times*, they're going to take something that's a little more staid—something that's a little bit more like what is normally considered a good comic—or a good novel. Looking at the *Time* list, about half of them are unrealistic like *Boulevard of Broken Dreams* or *Happy Clown* or *Bone*. I think with comics, there are certain things that comics do, that comics do *great*—and that you can't do in a novel. Something like *Bone*, you probably could do in a movie, but it's not the same. You can do fantasy things with drawings and convey them better in a comic than you can in a novel. I think that now that comics—graphic novels—have become a little bit more accepted, even just during the last three years, you see that these lists are starting to include things that have more "comic-ey" subject matter.

Caswell: Can you expand on that to talk about reading graphic novels versus reading a page of print?

Smith: Well, reading has the same rules—left to right, top to bottom. But when you read a comic, some of the information is in the picture. You do have to learn to read the pictures. You can't just look at the word balloons and skip to the next word. You've got to pick up the information and clues that are in the art. Comics have a very specific set of symbols that they've developed over the last sixty years, all their own, that you do need to know, that's a language unique to comics. Some of the rules are very simple—we all know that when somebody runs they leave a little cloud behind them.

Filipi: You're often quoted as saying that *Bone* is a Warner Bros.' cartoon meets *Lord of the Rings*, and when you go through *Bone*, I think one similarity to the Warner Bros.' cartoons is how often you include references to things outside of the world of the story, such as the inclusion of *Moby Dick* or, in a different way, the rat creatures loving quiche. There's a scene early on when Fone is emptying his backpack, and he has comic books in it and financial magazines and things like that. It's not unlike what the Warner Bros.' guys did in *What's*

Opera, Doc?—referencing Wagner. They were always referring to current events or popular music or "high" culture or even other Warner Bros.' stars. It just struck me how hard it must have been to keep that balance between very cartoony humor elements within a more serious fantasy world—maintaining humor but then also maintaining the threat that the characters face. And then it builds and builds and builds until it gets to the end of the story.

Smith: I think it was just a question of balance. Sometimes it would be very tempting to do something—especially if it was funny—to throw things off. I had to learn when it was appropriate to do so. If I knew a big serious event was coming in the story, I would back off on the cartoony stuff for a little while and bring the tone down, and then I could have a big hit. A good example of that is an eightpage story I did for *Disney Adventures Digest*, the kind of magazine you would find at the grocery store. That was a stand-alone story, but in my mind it was going to fit in with the continuity so that later when I collected the books for the graphic novel I could put it in there. The story was very cartoonlike, about the two Bone cousins, Fone Bone and Phoney Bone, finding a treasure map and following it. In four pages they get more beat up than in any other sequence I ever did—falling off cliffs and getting picked up by giant birds—and in the end it turns out that when they find the treasure, their dirty laundry is in there because Thorn had planted the treasure map since she knew she couldn't get them to do their laundry. It was a funny little bit and when it came time to put it into the books, it came right before a huge dramatic moment in the overall *Bone* story, where Fone Bone pulls out the little map that he found out in the desert. It turns out when he pulls that map out, we learn that it was drawn by Thorn. It proves that she has this past that's been hidden from her and the dragons are real. It really sets the whole story into motion—the whole rest of the story. When I printed that book, which was, I believe, the third *Bone* collection—in 1995, I think—I sat down, after the books were published, and read it. It didn't fit. On one page, there is a big *Mad Mad Mad Mad World* chase adventure, and then on the next page, Fone Bone pulls this map out of his backpack and initiates the most dramatic part of the story to date. I said, "Oh my gosh . . . I completely undercut it in so many ways." First of all, it's a treasure map, and I just made fun of all maps. So now he pulls out a treasure map, and the whole idea of finding a map has been turned into a cartoon joke. It was a completely silly, ridiculous story where they couldn't be killed no matter how many cliffs they fell off. All danger and drama were shown to be not real. They can't be harmed. So, I had to reprint the books and take that story out. That story just floats now and has no real home. That was a really long answer to your questions, but that's exactly what it is: you have to have balance. If there's comedy in the wrong place, it hurts it. But as long as it's in the right place, I think it actually gives the story speed and lightness that it really needs.

Filipi: Introducing the whole *Moby Dick* element is quite a digression. I'm wondering what the reaction has been over the years from fans. It's obviously something that's very important to you. It is something that you really wanted to be part of the story. It fits nicely with the cave where they're having the dreams, but it carries so much meaning with it—the characters from *Moby Dick*. How did you decide to include it?

Smith: In the beginning it was a comedy element, and it was part of that Warner Bros. nature of things that come from another world. I wanted Fone Bone to have things from this world because I wanted to impart to the readers that Boneville is like here. Part of the hook of *Bone* is that the humans are the fantasy and the cartoon characters are the reality. We identify with these little cartoony people as opposed to the humans. But as the joke went on, it began to carry some weight and filled a need: that the story had to show Fone Bone's inner life and his inner journey. It was perfect for that because it clearly meant something to the character in the story and it also is based on a book that is layered with symbolism. I thought that was a neat trick to use *Moby Dick* to show the symbolic layers in *Bone*. It became a signpost.

Filipi: Bartleby the rat cub refers to Melville too.

Smith: Yeah, it's just another reference.

Caswell: Can you talk about character development?

Smith: At first a character pops up, and you do need to work on a little background so that the character has some experience to build on. What I discovered is that I would bring in Gran'ma Ben, I knew her. I knew what kind of character she was, and I knew her personality. But as time passed she would grow and change. That new growth would reflect on her backstory. I created a backstory for her. She was the queen at one time and was hiding her granddaughter, á la *Sleeping Beauty,* in the woods to keep her safe. But that backstory necessitated certain personality traits. For example, she was very secretive—and uncommunicative. She had to be because she couldn't tell anybody about this, including Thorn. That led to her being this kind of overprotective character, which fed into her strength. So, I guess the development comes a little bit intellectually. You have to build, you have to write a back-story for the character.

Filipi: To follow up on that, it is amazing how quickly you become hooked on the characters in *Bone*. In the first fifteen pages, readers are presented with these characters that look very similar, they're simply drawn characters, and you're immediately concerned about what's going to happen to them.

Smith: That goes back to Schulz, too. In Schulz the characters pretty much look the same with just very small cues—costume cues—to tell you who they are. And with almost no ink the absolutely complete and complex range of human emotions is on every one of those *Peanuts'* characters' faces. But for you to just be able to pick up the story and read it and within just the first fifteen pages to know everybody, that's what you have to do when you're telling a story. You have to write it. I knew I had my three character types who were classic comedy types—you know, Groucho, Harpo, and Chico; Mickey, Donald, and Goofy; Jerry Seinfeld, George Costanza, and Kramer. I mean that type is something we all know, which has worked in comedy. But in order to engage the readers as quickly as possible, you have to set up a scenario and a back-and-forth dialogue that pull the readers in and lets them know who the characters are and give them situations to show their good and their bad sides, and their funny sides and sympathetic sides. That's just work. I wrote that first fifteen pages fifteen times, definitely, until I felt like the characters came across quick and clean—and that all that work was invisible. When you look at the *Mona Lisa,* you don't see all those layers that add to the depth and to the glow of the painting. You don't see that. You just look at it and go, "That's the best painting I've ever seen!"

Filipi: I read an interview with Charles Schulz and he said he thinks people are born with the ability to draw or they're not. He said you can work at it and you can improve your technique, but like singing, you're either able to do it or you're not. Do you agree with that?

Smith: Yeah, I do to a degree. I think it's a lot like a musical instrument, and you either have a predilection for it or you don't. And you have the patience and the drive to get better at it or you don't. I think that's actually probably very true. I do not think I could be a musician no matter how much I tried.

Filipi: *Shazam!* was a change of pace after *Bone,* in that you were writing for very well-known characters, like Captain Marvel, who have quite a bit of history. How did you get involved in the project and did you have any initial concerns about working with such iconic characters?

Smith: I got involved with *Shazam!* when the owners of the character, DC Comics, asked me to work on it. I think they felt the whimsy and drawing style of my *Bone* comics would fit the Big Red Cheese. I did have concerns. That character is loved by lots of people and I knew it would be difficult to please everyone, but I approached the project methodically. I researched the early comics and movie serials looking for the flavor and rhythms of the original stories, trying to figure out what it was that made Captain Marvel the most popular comic book character of the Golden Age in the 1940s and fifties. In the end, I decided it was the simple magical transformation of a small, helpless child into a super-being, able to bounce bullets off his chest and fly.

Caswell: To come back to the whole idea of inspiration, can you talk about *RASL* and the inspiration for that?

Smith: *RASL* is a story of an art thief—a guy whose life is not good. He's very discontented. I guess it's very important to point out that he's an interdimensional art thief. He has invented this spectral immersion suit, which includes large jet engines that he straps to his shoulders and his knees so that he can step in between universes, which he does for money. If someone's rich enough and they want the *Mona Lisa*, he'll go into another dimension and steal the *Mona Lisa*. *RASL* is very expensive. The inspiration for an idea like this is that I was interested in writing a comic about a character who is deplorable, as opposed to *Bone*, where the main character is very admirable and doesn't really think bad thoughts. He's not perfect, but he's basically a good guy. I wanted to do one where the hero was kind of a scoundrel. Another element of the interdimensional travel is that in order to operate these jet engines, and to successfully navigate in between the dimensional walls of the universes, Rasl, the main character, has to focus and concentrate and empty his mind—and have almost zen-like peace. However, the process of coming out of it is blinding white and hot and painful in a way that most humans wouldn't be able to take. So when he wakes up in the other dimension, he's on the floor screaming and it takes him days to recover. And there is a lot of drinking and smoking and gambling and whoring. Once he gets done with that, and gets that all out of his system, he gets to work on his next art theft. Then he has to start the process over again . . . in order to return, he has to undo all this. He has to cleanse himself—cleanse his body physically—no more smoking, no more drinking. So that's his life—stepping through the barrier. He goes into it clean and focused, and when he comes out of it he's a screaming wreck in pain. I'm not sure where the inspiration for that came from, but I do know that when I described the project to my wife, her first reaction was, "Oh, that's about the artistic process because that's what you're like every time you start a project and come out of it." Except for the gambling and whoring part. So who knows where these inspirations come from.

Filipi: Were there any other time-traveling works that have had a big influence on you?

Smith: No. Although I probably will try to look at some good time stories that exist out there. And the best ones are in *Star Trek*. But the time travel's not a huge element. It's more me ta physical. I'm very interested in physics, and string theory, and multiple universes. I have a good science. fiction centerpiece for this story: light is solid. If light is solid, that explains why light behaves as particles and as waves. It also explains why the speed of light is constant, because it doesn't really move. It's kind of like a giant surrounding essence. It's instantaneous. It explains all sorts of other little phenomenon. I thought it was a nice little nugget to have as a science-fiction artifact at the story's center even though it's completely nonsensical and not real. But that's Rasl's big discovery that allows him to do what he does and to step through dimensions.

Most of my influences for *RASL* are what I'm reading, like Stephen Hawking, Carl Sagan, all the literature that's out there that talks about the furthest, craziest ideas we have about multiple dimensions and that sort of thing. I love all that stuff. RASL will soon begin to wonder if the dimensions he's traveling to—he's stealing from—are real, or if he's creating them by going to them.

Filipi: When you're creating something that you know several different age groups are going to be reading, what things do you have to take into account? What considerations do you have to make? Or do you not even think about it, you're just trying to make the best story that you can?

Smith: I definitely don't categorize what's appropriate for one level and what's appropriate for another level. I just was always turned on by the kinds of stories that worked that way. Bugs Bunny cartoons—or even Disney feature films—work on both levels. One of the reasons parents can take their children to them is because the parents kind of like them, too. I mentioned *Huckleberry Finn* before and *Star Wars*—both of those are stories that are really pretty much for ten-year-old boys, right? They start off with Huck or Luke Skywalker, and they're swashbuckling, but as Huck goes on or as the *Star Wars* movies progressed, they became more sophisticated became more complex. And the stories had themes that were darker or about dealing with your father, in both *Huckleberry Finn* and *Star Wars*. So, it is those kinds of stories that get me excited, and that I want to try to do. I actually might have to wrestle with this a little bit more in *RASL* than I did in *Bone* because *RASL* does involve some more failings of the flesh type of subject matter. At this point I haven't actually started writing it yet, so I'm not sure where it's going to go. But my natural inclination as a writer is to tell adventure stories that operate for general audiences. We'll have to see. If RASL smokes and drinks too much, it may end up being a more adult work. But I don't know that yet. We'll have to see.

Filipi: In reading about you and other cartoonists, I'm always struck by how so many, almost without exception, seem to have a really strong sense of the people that came before them. In your work, you really get a sense of the people that you're influenced by, where I'm not sure you get the same sense of that when you're reading somebody's more autobiographical story, for instance. I'm wondering if you have a sense that, in a way, we're talking about two different traditions. There is more of a cartoonist tradition, where people are a little bit more acutely aware of artists like Winsor McCay and Herriman, Will Eisner, Jack Kirby, up until the present day, versus people that maybe aren't as interested in that trajectory, and that sequential art just happens to be the art that they're good at—as opposed to painting or. . . .

Smith: No, I think that Harvey Pekar, Robert Crumb, Art Spiegelman, and all those guys are unbelievably aware, and I would say even obsessed, with the tradition of cartooning that came before them. And Chester Brown. All those guys do absolutely feel like they can trace their roots through comics history, through Crumb, through Harvey Kurtzman, through George Herriman—very much the same way I would.

But I don't feel any need to conform to any rules of comics, as far as the industry or format is concerned. I broke many rules repeatedly and was told all along that everything I was doing was undermining everything that is good for comics, like collecting my books into graphic novels and putting them out while my number one was worth $300. People said, "If you do that, then you're going to make the number one comic worthless because you just made it available in a cheap format forever, and if you do that then the retailers are going to hate you because that's where they make their real money, in the back *issues*." So I was told you can't do graphic novels, you can't do collections, and I just didn't care about any of that stuff. So, when it comes to the artwork, I am deeply indebted and in awe of everybody who came before me. But in terms of traditions and industry, I haven't the slightest interest at all in that.

Filipi: Imagine a teenage girl or boy who might be completely unaware of the history and tradition of comic books. Yet, instead of writing in a journal they create a graphic record of what they're going through, completely outside of the trajectory we've been discussing.

Smith: There may be a generation right now . . . we call it the indie comics . . . where people are getting into it who may not have grown up reading certain people—or even knowing who they are. But these artists see the medium in a new way, which is very exciting to me, because even just ten years ago it seemed impossible that the medium could be so well known that people would flock to it and think that it is a place that they could do their art. But that could be happening now. And if it is, I would be excited.

Caswell: What do you think about the whole conundrum—how do you learn your craft and your art if you don't have a way to judge what is good and not good and the traditions on which the genre is based?

Smith: I actually think that's why most cartoonists who have come from comic books know the traditions. I mean, the ones that don't know them, really study them, and those who aren't dedicated to that level are going to drop off. You know that's going to happen. But the guys that make it, like Craig Thompson, they know what they're drawing. They've been reading comics, and they're picking the stuff that's good, and they're usually extremely knowledgeable about world comics—not just the stuff you can buy at the grocery store. There have to be, because you can't go to school to become a comic book artist. Well, I guess you can now. But it's rare. It is still up to the cartoonists to learn it themselves by finding the examples that turn them on. And boy they have them now. There's every kind of comic. There are autobiographical comics, comics about world geopolitics . . .

We are at a time in comics that is completely unlike any that has gone before, where we have a radical shift that involves many elements. There's the graphic novel, which started about twenty years ago with *Maus* and *The Dark Knight Rises* and has really come into flower recently with the wholesale acceptance of graphic novels by large chain bookstores like Barnes & Noble, Borders, and Amazon.com. There's also the element of the Internet, which takes the idea of underground comics and indie comics, which I just mentioned, to a whole new level. You don't even have to figure out how to get your comic books distributed or printed. All you have to do is understand your tools and your technology, and you can upload. There is a large and very healthy community that communicates with each other on the Internet. And the Internet is developing its own sets of symbols and languages that incorporate all that went before it.

The teenager you mentioned a minute ago, creating her graphic diary in her room, is exposed to all these things. The introduction of this new technology so deeply into our lives is making that change. I meet people all the time who are on the fan sites. Another element that's changing comics as we speak is manga, which has more in common with traditional American comics like superheroes, in my opinion, because of the factory nature of the production. Manga are commercial products, designed to sell numbers. For the most part, there is an artist and a writer assigned to create a product, although there are auteurs who transcend that. But the numbers are unprecedented. Manga are now at least fifty percent of all comics published in the U.S.—if not sixty, and the numbers are just growing. Manga are turning comics into a mass medium on the level of bestsellers, paperbacks, TV, movies. So, we're at a really interesting time. And I'll add one more element that is happening right now, and that's the acceptance by teachers, librarians, and the art world of this as an art form.

Caswell: Another component is the fact that manga have appealed to young girl readers. Comic books have historically appealed to boys. And these people are going to grow up. And I think as they grow up they're going to be a new generation of consumers for this art form in a way that we haven't had before.

Smith: And I'm very excited about it. I think that there are artists getting into this field every day and finding just what you're saying: that it's a fairly natural way to communicate—putting all the words and pictures together. I think that by the time this generation of manga artists grows up, the art is going to be there for everybody. That made me think of an Art Spiegelman story. I think I heard him tell it when he was speaking at Ohio State one time. He was describing the process of ingesting a comic, that these words and picture combinations that are almost instantaneously swallowed into your id through both sides of your brain, that the word and picture bursts that go down before your defenses can stop them, and they're in. I think that was one of the things that excites me about comics—as a kid and now as an artist using that medium. It reaches both sides of your brain and goes in deep and fast and is absorbed into your system almost before your conscious level can filter it. It's that fast. It's dangerous.

Paul Williams Interviews Jeff Smith

PAUL WILLIAMS / 2007

Paul Williams and James Lyons's *The Rise of the American Comics Artist: Creators and Contexts.* Jackson: University Press of Mississippi, 2010. Reprinted with permission.

To date, Jeff Smith's commercial success and critical attention has concentrated on his black-and-white bimonthly series *Bone,* published by Cartoon Books. *Bone* narrates the adventures of the three Bone cousins, who are slowly drawn into the political machinations and history of a valley filled with humans, dragons, rat creatures, talking bugs, and other fantastical beings. Based in Columbus, Ohio, Cartoon Books is an example of the creator-owned comics companies the self-publishing movement of the early 1990s was based on (Smith established Cartoon Books in July 1991, and his wife Vijaya Iyer is credited as publisher of Smith's comics).

It would not be an exaggeration to say that *Bone*'s success as a self-published comic was unprecedented and unmatched in the 1990s. Further, that success took place in an industry experiencing profound economic uncertainty. In 1993, American comics sales peaked at one billion dollars, but from 1995 onwards sales fell dramatically; inflation, the evaporation of comic book speculation purchases by investors, and Marvel's ill-judged acquisition of various comic-and non-comic-related assets were some of the reasons later cited (Wright 2003, 283).

In 1995 Smith decided to publish *Bone* through Image Comics to safeguard and extend his book's ability to be distributed to comics shops. Image had been established in 1993 as a partnership between various creators who left Marvel in order to publish their own comics featuring characters they created and owned. Smith's tenure at Image was a short one, however, and according to former Image executive director Larry Marder, Smith returned to publishing *Bone* solely through Cartoon Books when it was clear that his production costs as a self-publisher were less than the fixed production costs incurred by publishing through Image (Dean 2000).

From 1993 onwards, the *Bone* comics have been reprinted in various formats: as a graphic narrative in its entirety, as a series of graphic novels collecting each of the nine chapters constituting the *Bone* narrative, and in smaller-sized, full-color books published by Scholastic, to name but three of its versions (it was first published in collected editions under the rubric *The Complete Bone Adventures*). Since *Bone*'s conclusion Smith's projects have included a miniseries featuring the original Captain Marvel, coediting Fantagraphics' new series of *Pogo* collections (Walt Kelly's seminal mid-twentieth-century comic strip), and in March 2008 the release of Smith's *RASL*, an ongoing bimonthly self-published black-and-white comic from Cartoon Books, featuring a dimension-jumping fine art thief.

The following is a summary of an interview conducted by telephone on December 4, 2007. Initially the interviewer asserted how *The Rise of the American Comics Artist* was exploring a transformation in the perception of comics in the press, in universities, and in the wider reading public since the late 1980s, before mentioning some of the writers discussed in this collection, such as Chris Ware and Jim Woodring.

Jeff Smith: What happened in the last twenty years was down to a lot of the people you named, who were outside the mainstream at the time, but doing what basically became graphic novels. Will Eisner and a few others were trying to get people to call them graphic novels, but even in the early 1990s we were more likely to call them collections or trade paperbacks.

Paul Williams: You raise the issue of graphic novels: *Bone*'s been available in a few different formats: the *Complete Bone Adventures*, and then you had the nine books [publishing each chapter of the story together].
Smith: OK, well, from the beginning I saw *Bone* as a 1,300-page novel: *Huckleberry Finn* meets *Moby Dick*. I knew the story would have to be tight, and have a beginning, a middle, and an end, but in a marketplace driven by pamphlets—monthly or bimonthly chapter books—the story also had to be exciting and accessible for the reader. The question I asked myself was, "How do I keep this story available for the reader?" If this is a single, giant story, how do you keep the first chapter available for new readers? At that time there was not really a trade paperback or graphic novel market. There was a back issue market, which was a big part of the economy of that time for comic stores. But with back issues, once they are sold, they're gone. You can't buy that comic any more.

So after a series of false starts, I was still experimenting to see how people would take to complete collections. Some comic companies, such as Kitchen

Sink and Fantagraphics (with their complete *Krazy Kat*), were entering this market. So I took a block of six issues for a year of *Bone* and collected them into a book. After three of those, I could see that the natural rhythm of the story didn't go in six-issue chunks. Some arcs, or chapters, were only five issues long or eight or nine issues by the end. After the third *Complete Bone Adventures* collections, I scrapped that version and repackaged the story in books that felt like chapters. Having scrapped the *Complete Bone Adventures*, I gave the collections new titles. So the first chapter when the Bone cousins are run out of Boneville was titled, "Out of Boneville." But the idea was always a one-volume edition. Fortunately the technology appeared to make this possible when the story was finished; otherwise I don't know how I would have had the whole thing bound!

The collections were obviously going to affect the store owners' ability to resell back issues. Me and other indy creators would sit around at conventions, and this could be Glasgow or Oakland, we would have long discussions about whether there was a market for these books. The comic business didn't seem to operate like other businesses. I didn't understand why a comic store didn't work like a hardware store, where if you sell out of a hammer you restock the hammer. But with comics, if you sell out of something you can't order any more. I can't think of any other industry like that. If I go into a music store, I can't imagine not being able to buy *The White Album*; if you go into a bookstore, you can always buy *Moby Dick*. But in the early 1990s, you couldn't buy *Superman* #1! Neil Gaiman was just starting to collect *The Sandman* into books. We were browbeaten by retailers thinking we were undercutting their profit, but we pointed out that the profit margin on an eleven dollar book was better than a comic that cost two dollars, three dollars. And with a book, if it sells you can restock it, and it's even more profitable. We would talk about this all the time, Scott McCloud and I.

Williams: I was hoping you would say a little more about that really, because it was controversial. It seems so commonplace now but fifteen years ago it wasn't that well heard of. Was there much browbeating?
Smith: Oh yes. In the mid-to-late 1990s, I did an interview with *Comics Retailer* magazine, and I referred to a revolution in format. This put the interviewer on edge; they were upset by the word "revolution." Discussing the idea that the marketplace would turn upside down was frightening.

Williams: What do you think the status of back issues is now, given that things really have gone 180 degrees? Walking past the local comic shop, the things they have in the window are graphic novels or trade paperbacks. You really have to dig for the comics now.

Smith: I was trying to get out of the back issue market but I succeeded too well in getting *Bone* into other markets and being a "book." My next project is going to be released in issues: this thing is for comic stores.

Williams: It sounds like you already have firm ideas about how your next project, *RASL*, will be serialized and collected together at the end.

Smith: Of course. I wrote out a business plan in 1989, before I started self-publishing *Bone*. You kind of have to, it goes alongside the creative process. If you were making a movie you would have to plan it out completely before it started. Way ahead of the ending I knew how the story was going to conclude.

Williams: How far do you see the success of *Bone* as your success in finding viable distribution deals at pivotal times in the history of the industry? It is not as if comics have been an unmitigated success story in the last few years—the industry is so convulsive it is often hard to track. It seems to me one of the reasons for Cartoon Books' success is in the negotiation of those distribution pitfalls that have put many companies and comic shops out of business.

Smith: The reason why *Bone* was a perfect thing for me is because I wasn't a publisher trying to find commercial properties. With *Bone*, I had lived with it for so long it was more like having a child and finding places for it to go. But I didn't want it to starve: it wasn't that we said, "There's a door here, let's go through it," but "Let's make a door to go there."

With the libraries, *Bone* switched to hardcover editions when we moved from the *Complete Bone Adventures*. The durability of hardcover editions made it more friendly to librarians, and they played a large role in *Bone*'s success, getting the book into the hands of children. That would have been impossible to do in the comic book-directed marketplace. So in terms of distribution being part of *Bone*'s success, that was a big part of it! *The Superman* and *Spider-Man* comics, they sold to a certain collector type, a certain type of reader obsessed with certain details about the character, and their vulnerabilities or whatever. And then there are underground comix, whatever you want to call them, that are a broader genre, including serious autobiography, and the kind of fantasy that Jim Woodring and I do.

Williams: Do you want to say a little about the difficulties involved in trying to promote comics as a credible artistic medium, while at the same time young readers through the libraries have been a big part of *Bone*'s success story? Are you very conscious of the balancing act there, between promoting comics for their literariness, as a viable artistic medium, while aware of the fact that popularity comes from a universal audience?

Smith: First, I don't think something that's universal should be shallow or without artistic merit. In terms of negotiating, there wasn't much to do. Through the libraries the book was being read by children and their parents, by parents to their children, and then by parents on their own. This was happening without my knowledge; librarians were putting it on their must-read lists. By about 2002, the graphic novel seemed to be making money in Barnes and Noble and FNAC [two entertainment store chains]. By 2004 to 2005—and I think manga was a big part of this, because they made graphic novels a profit center for book stores—at this time there was a big enough body of work to start stocking shelves, so you could have a whole section of graphic novels. I don't have to tell you which, you know the ones I mean, the twelve books everyone can name!

As for publishing comics as an art form, any piece of literary symbolism I'm aware of I can put into *Bone*. It doesn't matter whether kids get it or not, but it's there.

Williams: How do you feel about comics, and your work in particular, becoming the subject of academic study? Being put on reading lists, say, or lectures being given on it on twenty-first-century literature courses?

Smith: I'm ambivalent about it. I mean, I won't lie, I am rejoicing in the serious acceptance. But part of me, the part that got into comics when I was nine, is thinking, "Did we actually manage to make comics boring?" But I do love the dignity comics have now. Back in the early 1990s Scott McCloud and I would talk a lot about how it was unbelievable these great comics were things that weren't taught. That was a good time to sit in the bar at conventions getting drunk and discussing comics at midnight.

Williams: In that short space of time since the early 1990s it seems the whole field and the status of creators has changed. Do you feel that the battle for respectability is over?

Smith: Almost. It's partly over. Back then we treated it as a lost cause. Gary [Groth] and Kim [Thompson] at Fantagraphics had a lot to do with the fact that it wasn't. Most people's attitude at the time was you just do it—you do it for the people that get it. You didn't do it for kids, you did it for cartoonists. I did it for me and other people that got it. But as for the current levels of respectability—I didn't think it was possible! With *Bone*, I knew the medium could handle it, a full-length story; that it could be read by more people than were reading it. I often get requests from professors for information, so somebody is getting it—I like that.

Williams: In terms of the medium, it seems alongside the consolidation of graphic novels there has been a raiding of the archive and bringing to light a hundred years of comic creators. Can you say a little about your involvement with Fantagraphics and the republication of Walt Kelly's *Pogo*? I am tempted to say now is the best time to be reading comics because you can get hold of comics you simply couldn't have got hold of five years ago, let alone twenty, thirty years ago.

Smith: I've been saying this for years, Paul—it just keeps getting better. I stated this in *Bone*. When I got hold of the complete *Popeye*, I had never seen all of them. To see all of them, to get a feel of it together . . . it was like when Fantagraphics republished *Krazy Kat*. I knew who these artists were, I had seen their work in different places, but now you had a resource you can draw on. The complete *Peanuts* was long overdue, because by the end of the run you forgot how good the early stuff is.

My involvement with *Pogo* began with Fantagraphics republishing Walt Kelly's *Our Gang*, which was based on *The Little Rascals* films. They are not that fantastic. But it's still Walt Kelly, right? With the republication of *Pogo*, it has been slow going because Kelly's syndicate did not survive [unlike *Peanuts's* syndicate]. That means it has been a longer story to get good, acceptable prints. Each book will contain about two years of material. It is all being published from the start for the same thing happened to *Pogo* that happened to *Peanuts*—you don't remember how good the early ones are! They hold up really well. That first year is so funny. And as we get into the early McCarthy era, that material is so relevant today. So working on this project is Gary Groth, me, and Carolyn Kelly, Walt's daughter.

Williams: As a sense of twentieth-century comics solidifies into a real history of comics with its big figures being put back into place, is there anyone you think is due a revival? Do you think the world of comics has forgotten some people that should be remembered?

Smith: For me, Walt was the last one. The greats for me are Barks, Schulz, and Kelly. I do think that Joe Kubert needs a monster book. He is a different kind of figure altogether, but a great comic artist whose work should be collected. Of course, he drew comic books.

Williams: That's interesting because the people who are being republished are primarily known for their comic strip work.

Smith: Yeah, I think cartoon strips are where the most interesting work was being done in comics in its first one hundred years. The big work being done today is in comics and graphic novels. This is partly because the space the newspapers dedicate to strips is shrinking and the strips are getting smaller.

Williams: Are there strip artists you read today? Do you still turn to the funny pages?

Smith: Actually, I think *Dilbert* is a funny comic strip. My brother works in a partitioned office so he doesn't think so! Apart from that, the only recent comic strip I have been impressed with is *Calvin & Hobbes*. Y'know, this wasn't what I was expecting to be talking about!

Williams: Well we are interested in an industrial point-of-view. One of the ways we are approaching the field of comics is from a cultural studies background, so we are particularly interested in the material text, production and distribution, and similar issues. Do you often talk to academics, and do you have an idea about what academics do with comics?

Smith: The kind of people I talk with are, say, librarians writing about graphic novels. Also, high school-level teachers, who are finding they can get people who won't read anything to read *Bone*.

I started out on two tracks: to create the art and to get people interested in the story, but to finish it I had to make sure it made money. I did not try to get rich but I did want to make enough money to get to the end of the story! By putting a spine on the story you look at it as something more real. It structures that work by fitting it into the spine of the graphic novel. It needs a beginning, a middle, and an end spoken in a single voice. I rarely read collections of superhero comics produced by a team of creators—actually, except for that 1960s *Fantastic Four* stuff.

When I go to talk in schools, or to any group in fact (and I get invited to talk to all kinds of groups: national librarians' conferences, managers of Borders, universities, high schools), I give a very similar talk to all of them. I say that comics are a literary art form: the smallest unit of a comic is any two given panels. You need that to make time elapse and for actions to occur. You read it left-to-right and top-to-bottom, like a prose page. The other thing I talk about is the graphic novel itself, the form. When I talk about the art itself I refer to my symbolism.

For instance, I use water as a symbol. This because I'm a *Moby Dick* and *King Arthur* fan. When Arthur comes across any fountain surrounded by women in the middle of the woods you know something good is going to happen! In *Bone,* water signals that an important point has been reached in the story: when Fone Bone enters the valley in "Out from Boneville" [the first chapter of the *Bone* narrative], he leaps from the waterfall; when he is being chased, he says, "Stupid, stupid rat creatures!" while he is suspended on a branch by the waterfall; when he first meets Thorn, she is bathing in a stream. The Dragon comes out of a well when Fone Bone goes to fetch water from it, and at the end of the story, when the water is rushing by, all the dragons come out in the flood, that kind of thing. Like *Huckleberry Finn,* water is an integral part of the story's symbolism.

Williams: I am enthused to hear you talk about the two together, these two tracks, because I find that even very good students who have no problems tucking into *Huckleberry Finn* do find reading comics unusual. I don't mean from the position of "Why are you giving us a comic instead of a book?" but literally the act of reading—you do need to practice it. If you are brought up reading comics it is easy to forget that if you are not brought up reading comics they are actually quite alien ways of telling a story, and you can't just throw students a comic and say, "Look at the symbolism." The eye has to be trained to read the comic and the symbolism in a symbiotic relationship.

Smith: I remember sitting around at a convention, and some of the older cartoonists, like Sergio [Aragonés], or Mark Evanier, were telling the story of how they had gone, as a group, to Africa on an official visit. They were showing comics to people who had never seen them ever before. And they were asked the question, "Why does this character have no legs here?" when the cartoonist had gone in for a medium shot. This was probably in the 1960s, so perhaps these first-time readers were not really familiar with the vocabulary of television or film images more generally, like the long-shot or the close-up. No, now I think I might have read this story in Mark Evanier's book! Wherever I came across this story, I think it shows that comics do operate as a language you have to learn to become fluent in.

Williams: It does sound like you see a great deal of continuity between *Bone* and other Great American Novels, say *Huckleberry Finn* and *Moby Dick*. Did you have that in mind as you were executing it?
Smith: Without trying to be pretentious, I was trying to do something like Melville does in *Moby Dick*, which is a book I enjoy reading for the sheer act of reading. The book spends so much time when nothing is happening with the story, but for the reader it is a pleasure just being in the presence of the

author. I think that is why it has never been a really good movie. There are also its layers and layers of symbolism. I did try to get a *Moby Dick* style of narration where you just stay with the story because of the pleasure of being in its company.

If we are dignifying issues as chapters, *Huckleberry Finn* was perfect for the overall structure. It starts like a boy's adventure story (which I enjoy anyway) like *Tom Sawyer*—it has the start of a swashbuckling boy's adventure, but goes on to get darker and more sophisticated as the story progresses. When I was reading *Uncle Scrooge* written and drawn by Carl Barks, I wished there was an Uncle Scrooge story that was as long as *Huckleberry Finn* and *The Odyssey*, which is where *Bone* came from. I hope it worked.

WORKS CITED

Dean, Michael. 2000. "The Image Story." *The Comics Journal.* http://archives.tcj.com/3
_online/n_image4.html [accessed 12 Mar. 2010].

Wright, Bradford W. 2003. *Comic Book Nation.* Rev. ed. Baltimore: John Hopkins University Press.

Thorn comic strip that appeared in The Ohio State University's *The Lantern* (1982).

Thorn comic (1986).

Bone in full color (2005).

Bone in full color (2005).

Shazam!: The Monster Society of Evil (2007).

Little Mouse Gets Ready (2009).

Smiley's Dream Book (2018).

RASL in full color (2018).

Tüki: Save the Humans (2014).

Cartoonist Jeff Smith Rocks the World of Graphic Novels

LINDA M. CASTELLITTO / 2008

BookPage (February 2008). Reprinted with permission.

Jeff Smith recently returned from a world tour, an endeavor most often as-
sociated with religious leaders or rock stars. Smith won't be riding in a pope-
mobile any time soon, but he's got Bono-worthy status in the world of comic
books and graphic novels. The writer-artist didn't harbor dreams of having
fans worldwide when he began drawing his *Bone* comics. Nor did he suspect
that his work would someday be published by Scholastic, which launched its
new Graphix imprint with the *Bone* books. The latest entry in the nine-volume
series, *Bone: Ghost Circles*, is out this month. Smith spoke to *BookPage* from
Columbus, Ohio, the home base of Cartoon Books, which he launched in 1991
to self-publish the *Bone* books (his wife, Vijaya, became his business partner
in 1992).

"I started *Bone* pretty much in the garage, writing and drawing a black-
and-white comic every couple of months and putting it into the comic-book
market, for other cartoon-heads," he recalls. "I definitely wasn't picturing them
as children's books."

Instead, he wanted to create comics with characters reminiscent of the
ones he'd loved as a kid—Uncle Scrooge, Bugs Bunny—and with storylines he
craved, but could never find. "We always think of comics as a kind of ephemeral
thing," he explains. "They're in the newspaper every day, and Charlie Brown
never gets to kick the ball or change his shirt. I always thought the medium of
comics could handle a really large story with a large structure." Smith drew a
daily newspaper cartoon when he was a student at the Ohio State University
and, after college, he founded an animation studio. But his interest in creating
a more substantive story never waned. Then, in the mid-1980s, "I discovered

the indie underground comic book world . . . a movement where people were drawing their own comics and telling their own stories."

For twelve years, Smith created his story: 1,300 pages via fifty-plus issues of *Bone*. The epic story focuses on the adventures of Fone Bone, Phoney Bone, and Smiley Bone. The cousins are little blobby guys who, despite their small size and adorable appearance, prove to be quite strong. This is fortunate, because the Bones keep encountering scary creatures that want to eat them. They also have to climb over mountains, dash through dark forests and reason with dragons as they journey through unfamiliar territory rife with unusual beings, dark magic, and other surprises. Smith encountered his own surprise when he began talking with Scholastic—namely, the suggestion that the *Bone* series be published in color. Smith says that, when he first created *Bone*, he stuck with black-and-white for several reasons, including a small budget, an affinity for newspaper comics and his desire to pay tribute to Art Spiegelman's Pulitzer Prize-winning graphic novel memoir, *Maus*. It's a bit, well, comical how things turned out: Spiegelman was instrumental in convincing Smith to add color to the *Bone* books. (Spiegelman and his wife, Françoise Mouly—art editor of *The New Yorker*—were advising Scholastic on the imprint-launch.)

"At first, I thought the idea was a little sketchy, that it would be like colorizing *Casablanca*," Smith says, adding that he's not comparing *Bone* to the classic movie. "But then, I felt we could do storytelling things with color: create depth, direct people's eyes, create a mood. If something is happening at sunset or twilight, you can only tell the reader or draw really long shadows [in black-and-white]. But if you throw a bright orange light on it, you can really change it. I've been won over." And the books have won over young readers. Smith's cartoon-head fans share the books with their own children, but he says librarians deserve a lot of credit for getting the *Bone* books into kids' hands, too.

"Librarians and teachers have let me know they are getting reluctant readers to read with *Bone*. So people can actually see there are benefits to graphic novels, vs. the stigma that always was attached to comics . . . I knew it wasn't true. I learned to read because of comics." Smith says he loved reading about Tarzan and Sherlock Holmes when he was younger; he later turned to *The Iliad*, *The Odyssey*, *Le Morte d'Arthur*, and *Moby-Dick*. "I really like epics. *Moby-Dick* is honestly my favorite book. I'm just fascinated by the literary structure," he says. He cites *The Adventures of Huckleberry Finn* as an influence, too: "It was a real model for me. It starts off very much like a boy's adventure story, but it quickly grows darker and the themes become more complicated and sophisticated." *Bone: Ghost Circles* has no small amount of darkness; Smith says the book is the beginning of the final act. "A volcano has loosed ghost circles: vast areas that are too poisonous to enter. It's the darkness before the dawn."

The Bones and their friends must make their way past the circles, battling thirst, fear, and confusion about the Moby Dick costumes they suddenly seem to be wearing. There's plenty of humor amid the scary, suspenseful storylines and—while eager readers can quickly devour the story, thanks to lots of dialogue—they'll surely be slowed by drawings that feel as if they're moving or, in some cases, breathing. It's that inimitable mix of art plus story that makes graphic novels so stimulating and engaging, Smith says. "As an author, I'm extremely aware every day that, when it comes down to it, you read [graphic novels] left to right, top to bottom, just like a book. They have their own subsets of symbols that don't belong to prose and movies—it is its own visual art form that works on its own and makes an immediate connection with a reader."

The success of *Bone* has brought Smith a new level of respect, even from his own family. "One really fun thing that's changed [since Scholastic began publishing the books] is that my parents and their friends' kids know about *Bone* now," he says. "Before, it was only in the comic-book stores, but now it's in bookstores. All of a sudden, my parents are like, 'Oh, my gosh!'"

Holiday Interview

TOM SPURGEON / 2012

The Comics Reporter (January 5, 2012). Reprinted with permission.

The year 2011 was the twentieth year anniversary for *Bone*, Jeff Smith's well-loved fantasy epic that has enjoyed successful runs in serial comics form, in trade paperback form, in massive collections, in *color* serial volumes aimed at the slightly unlikely audience of North American schoolchildren, and now in a deluxe, full-color, under-one-cover format. I remain very fond of *Bone*. I'm particularly taken by how lightly Smith pushes theme in a genre where theme is worn—literally—like armor. *Bone* works as both an extended, pleasurable, action-adventure story and for its almost casual development of ideas such as how single instants of commitment and intimacy can alter lives, how bad decisions can be as important as good ones, and how we orient ourselves towards the idea and reality of home.

The Columbus, Ohio-based cartoonist has continued to put his comics chops on display in the series *RASL*, four years old this March. *RASL* combines science fiction with true science literature and, of all things, *noir*. The latest issue, #12, featured a classic, all-time information dump that related the story of Nikola Tesla while underscoring how dependent we are on narratives—personal, biographical, pulp—and narrators to help us figure out the truth. Smith is closing in on the final sequences of that book, and will finish the saga in the next few issues.

Smith has always been extremely supportive of this site and my work generally, for which I'm forever grateful. It was fun to catch up with him on the phone in early December.—*Tom Spurgeon*

Tom Spurgeon: Did you get a chance to reflect on the occasion of this year's anniversary? Did you look back at all on how things have developed over the last twenty years? Was that a part of your year at all?

Jeff Smith: Actually, it was, but the year before. That's when I spent a lot of time thinking back. Vijaya and I were talking what we were going to do the next year. I knew our twentieth anniversary was coming up, so in 2010 we put our heads together to figure out what we could do to celebrate. We came up with this idea for the color one-volume edition. Make it deluxe. We have the absolute-type thing, and we have the fancy one with the gold coin and all of that stuff. I had to write an essay and do a timeline. That really made me reflect on the last twenty years. I was kind of amazed looking back on it. Twenty years is a lot of time. You can do a lot of shit in twenty years. [*laughter*]

So I did spend quite a bit of time in reflection.

Spurgeon: Did anything pop out at you from that twenty years, maybe something you hadn't thought of before?

Smith: One thing that popped out at me that I hadn't really thought about was some of the bad times. [*laughs*] You kind of move past those and keep moving.

Spurgeon: Is there an example of a bad time? Because your career path looks pretty positive from the outside-in.

Smith: [*laughs*] Well, good. I'm glad. [*laughter*] 2001 was a bad year for me. We had a lot of money troubles. I got into these rows with Dave Sim and Linda Medley, and it was very demoralizing. I forgot how close we came to going out of business. We put a bunch of money into toys—toys were really big—in 1999 and 2000. We didn't lose any money in the long run, but it tied up a whole bunch of money for a long time. Then the problems we had with Linda. I was slowing down my output right around that time, because I was getting into the heavy parts of the story and it was hard to write. Just a lot of factors came together. I forgot how tough that was. We had to let all our employees go. We had to leave our office. I completely forgot that there was a year when Vijaya and I and Kathleen—Kathleen Glosan, our production manager—the three of us were all in my one-room studio above the garage trying to survive. Eventually we did.

Spurgeon: Was it just a matter of getting the book out until the money situation improved? Did you . . . stop fighting with people? [*laughter*] Did people stop fighting with you? What led you out of the desert?

Smith: I don't know, man. I don't know why I got into fights with people that year. I didn't feel like I was fighting with people. I just mostly felt like people were getting upset with me. I don't know. We just had to tighten our belts in the hopes we could ride it out, and eventually we did. We were smarter about things. We stopped doing the toys, obviously. That was silly. We were always thinking about ways to repackage the books. Eventually we pulled it together.

Spurgeon: People might be astonished to hear that you went through that tough of a time, given your reputation for being very successful after *Bone* finally hit. That makes me wonder . . . do we underestimate the degree of difficulty in you getting where you are? People wonder at times why we don't see more people following the Jeff Smith model, why we don't see stories similar to yours.
Smith: [*laughs*] I'm sure I don't know the answer to why anybody else hasn't done it like that, except they're probably sane. [*laughter*] You're constantly battling with distributors, or people that aren't doing their job. It's a pretty big enterprise. You're dealing with printers that are sometimes overseas—sometimes they're in Michigan. You're dealing with licensing in foreign languages and suddenly a publisher goes out of business and hasn't paid you. It's fairly complicated.

Spurgeon: It seems like you're at a similar point right now, at least creatively, in terms of gearing up for a final push on *RASL*. Is it fair to say you're locking into that last phase on that series?
Smith: I *was* entering the final arc on *Bone* at that time. The final movement. It became very difficult because of how complicated the task is. And I am right there with *RASL* right now.

Spurgeon: Is it different this time around? Are things going more smoothly for having that earlier experience?
Smith: Well, I think so. It's surprisingly the same when it comes down to struggling to meet deadlines and tearing your hair out. I haven't gotten any better at that in twenty years. What's different is that after this long I have a team that's got my back. A really, really good team. Obviously Vijaya has been my partner since before my first issue. Vijaya and I actually came up with the plan together for Cartoon Books, to do a black and white comic book every two months and each one will be a chapter in this larger novel. Vijaya knew the ending of the story before we even started. I've got Kathleen, who I mentioned earlier, Kathleen Glosan, who's helped Vijaya run the office. She's the contact with most of the outside world. She sets up publicity, takes care of things, makes sure what I'm supposed to be doing. I've got Steve Hamaker, who does not only the color on *Bone* but about any art-related job that needs to be done at Cartoon Books that isn't actual comic book pages. I still have to do those by myself. And we

have Tom Gaadt, who does all the web stuff. He handles the store, and goes on the road. Everyone's been with us for years. We've had a good group for a long time.

Spurgeon: Tell me about the creative part of moving into a final chapter on a book like *RASL*. How much of it is figuring out the book in addition to deciding where you want to take it? How much is learning where the book wants to take you?
Smith: I start out thinking I know what the ending is and where I'm going. And I do. Mostly. The ending will be the same ending. But as you write, especially a serialized book, which is what comic books do really well, I think, the story grows. You get ideas as you're going along. In *RASL*, there's that spooky little girl that doesn't talk. She was not in my original plan. She just kind of popped onto the page one time. I was suggesting that Rasl, by going to different universes and traveling back and forth, was altering something. He was messing with nature. It popped into my head that it would be super-creepy and really freaky that this little girl would be standing there that can't talk. She's taken her place in the comic and has grown and is now going to be part of the ending. I'm a little nervous about the ending I came up with for her, because it's a little intense. I think I'm going to do it anyway.
    Does that answer your question?

Spurgeon: It does. And you're close enough we might see this in the next year or year and a half, right?
Smith: Yeah, I'm shooting to have it done by next summer. Here's what's weird, though. My original plan was to have it done in nine issues. Then I expanded that to fifteen issues because the story kind of got bigger. Now I wonder if I can fit it into fifteen. I'm really close. It's either going to be fifteen or sixteen or maybe fifteen will have forty-eight pages. It's kind of embarrassing to admit that it's that unplanned, that out of control. [*laughs*] But that's the way I lay into these projects, and see what happens.

Spurgeon: You and I talked a bit about this yesterday, setting up this phone call: you mentioned that when you utilize certain genres that the way the lead is oriented within them restricts your narrative a bit. Specially, the hallmarks of one of the genres you're using, *noir*, limits the readers' information to what the lead knows.
Smith: Yeah.

Spurgeon: Can you talk about the challenges there? When you mentioned that you used to switch perspective in *Bone*, this wasn't a particular memory I had of that story. But when I looked, I found you did do that rather frequently. And now with *RASL,* you can't. We've been in this guy's pocket for the whole trip.
Smith: It's one of the tropes of *noir* that I didn't think through when I committed to this project. [*laughs*] I've had a lot of fun. *RASL* kind of gestated in my mind, Tom, for about eight years. While I was finishing *Bone*, while I was finishing *Shazam!* . . . I finally got into it and had a lot of fun reading Dashiell Hammett and reading Raymond Chandler and watching movies. Just getting into that hardboiled thing. Figuring out here's my character, and here's the triangle. Plus I was getting into the physics. I was doing all that, and then it got down to finally writing the comic. Then I realized you can only know what the main hero knows.

So as you were alluding to, in *Bone* I can just cut away to the bad guys. I can show what the Hooded One and Kingdok are talking about and plotting against the Bones. Add tension that way. Or if I finished up a bit with Fone Bone and Thorn, I could cut to the shenanigans of Smiley and Phoney. That way it would never get boring. You could hop around and see what everyone else was doing. Then I started *RASL,* and in *noir* you can't know . . . RASL is in *every frame.* You *only* know what he knows, and that's incredibly difficult. I can't just set up the plot and have exposition done by a villain. It all has to be uncovered by Rasl. It's a fun thing to read, and to watch in a movie; it's very difficult to write.

Spurgeon: Do you like Rasl? He's very different than the more iconic characters you used in *Bone.*
Smith: I like him. I like him a lot. I think he's very interesting. He's tough. He's a lot of things I wish I was. He's a lot of things I'm glad I'm not—he's a fuck-up. [*Spurgeon laughs*]

I started this series with him being portrayed as an art thief. I wanted the audience to meet him as a questionable character, and wonder what this guy is all about and can you sympathize with him. That's why I pushed the whole art thief/heist thing. He's not a goody two-shoes guy, that's for sure. As we uncover his past, we find out he was sleeping with his partner's wife. He's made all sorts of bad decisions. Some were on purpose, the kind of destruction he's left in his wake. I think slowly we're discovering that he did it all for a reason, even if it wasn't really well thought-out. We're finding out that the things he's rebelling against and fighting against were really powerful, bad things. We'll get more information on that even in these final chapters.

Spurgeon: When I think of your work with theme with *Bone*, I think of you putting together different elements from the genres with which you were working, but not really pushing a very specific lesson or moral. Certain themes very gently revealed themselves, and really had to be engaged by the reader. Is that also true of *RASL,* do you think? One thing that occurs to me is that a lot of what we see is him fixing things, fixing the situation, and a kind of redemption arc. But it's so delicate I'm not even sure about that. Do you think in terms of theme?

Smith: I do. Some things will drift to the surface, and you can decide to highlight them or not. But yeah, I definitely think of theme. My favorite book is *Moby Dick*. And it's a genre book. It's a high seas adventure book. But you can read it on many levels—I'm not saying anything new there, Tom. [*laughter*] But it's not an accident that it works that way. Melville really layered it in a certain way, and used symbolism—some of it heavy-handed, but some of it very subtle. It's meant to be open-ended. When you're working in genre and you're using those kind of symbols, the idea is not to give someone a lesson, but to leave these portals open for people to go into and experience the story and have it reflect something in their own lives and things they're going through. So even though the story has forward motion and has themes and arcs, the stories I like is where the themes are created specifically to be open to the reader. [*pause*] Did I say that very well? [*laughter*]

Spurgeon: I sometimes wonder how people are reacting to *RASL*. You know, *Bone* had this thing where it started out as this pastoral, Walt Kelly/Carl Barksish comedy and then pulled itself together into this full-blown fantasy, taking readers to a different place entirely than where they started. Even so, I could sort of guess how people were reacting to it. But with *RASL*, I don't know. The only thing that comes up as a recurring element in the writing about it is that everyone notes that this is a more mature work—at least in that you're drawing naughty. [*Smith laughs*] Do you hear back from people? Are you surprised by anything you're heard about the work?

Smith: My favorite reaction was my friend Terry Moore. He wrote somewhere that it was weird to see a Jeff Smith drawing doing dirty things. [*laughter*] In terms of what I was picking up people started reading it eager to pick up on what I was doing? In the last year I'm definitely feeling a connection. I was talking to my Italian publisher, and he had said something very insightful that made me realize that he was really paying attention to it. He's my *Bone* publisher there; we haven't licensed *RASL* in any foreign languages yet, because we're waiting until it's done. The pages where I talk about Tesla, where I ruminate on Tesla for a while, he said, "Oh, that's the part of *Moby Dick* where he talks about the whale heads." That's exactly it. That's exactly what I'm doing. It's fun. It's connected to the story; it has something to do with it. But really I'm just doing that. I'm going to spend a couple of pages and talk about something I like that. Try to hypnotize people while they're reading it.

Spurgeon: Has this one been a struggle at all as a publisher? The industry is different now, and you're doing it in multiple formats—you like the serial format, and a lot of people have given up on serial publishing. Has it been difficult at all as a publisher to get this one out there?

Smith: A little bit. I don't see it getting the kind of traction that *Bone* got. On the other hand, I've only been doing it for three years. *Bone* was three years in before it got any traction itself. But yeah, it's been a little bit of a struggle. I've thrown a couple of formats out there just to see what people want. I got some push back on the over-sized volumes. I did those large, album-sized volumes. I liked them. But people were *not* liking them. So we tried the pocket book. And that got some reviews, in *Publishers Weekly*. Some of the reviews actually said, specifically, "Oh, this solves the problem of this stupid, over-sized things that doesn't fit in my bookshelf and my longbox." So okay: that's who I made the pocket book for.

Spurgeon: Do you get any sense that people's consumption habits are different now? People have told me that even if a new comic had the exact level of appeal that say, *Bone* had, that structurally you might not be able to do another *Bone*. The market is just wholly resistant to many of the factors that made *Bone* a hit. Do you have any sense of that?

Smith: I don't, Tom, to be honest. I don't really see what's so different about right now. What would be different? That Marvel and DC are trying to swamp the shelves and wipe everything else out? That's the same as it was back then.

Spurgeon: One thing that might be different is you have fewer similar books on the stands now.

Smith: There weren't too many back then, either. [*laughter*] There never were that many. And even all together we weren't that big of a deal. I think if a comic book showed up and had that spark, I don't see why somebody couldn't do it. *RASL*'s obviously not that one. [*laughter*] It's doing all right. This issue #12, the one that just shipped, the numbers started to go up again. So I don't think it's that different. It's just that it's still fucking hard.

Spurgeon: What's your digital footprint like on *RASL*? I probably should have researched that before we talked. [*Smith laughs*] But are you publishing that way?

Smith: I'm getting my toes wet. We worked with comiXology to develop two stand-alone apps: one for *Bone* and one for *RASL*. And that went very well. *RASL* sold just as well as *Bone* that way. That was exciting to see. We're developing books for the book readers with a couple of companies. We're still gathering information. We're using comiXology to see *how* people are buying. It looks to me like comiXology is trying to move the—what am I trying to say?—it looks to me like they're replicating the direct market into the digital arena. They're a digital comic bookstore. They're selling comic books, and they're hoping people will come back and buy them and they'll feed the habit the same way. The same thing comic book stores are doing. I bet there are other ways to get your digital comic out there. There are some decisions still to be made, I think.

Spurgeon: You're talking basic decisions . . .?

Smith: Yes. Right now there are comic books where you get a new issue every month. There are books—the readers, everyone's got at least one. Then there are the apps. There's quite a bit still out there to be done digitally that hasn't been done yet. We're looking into it. We're going to spend some time to get it right. But we think it's a way for self-publishing to really work.

Spurgeon: So if you figured out your 2011 in 2010, have you figured out your 2012 yet? Do you know what's next? Do you have a next creative project?

Smith: I've got the next two years kind of mapped out, the big events I want to hit. One of them is a new project. The one I'm doing after *RASL*. It's still too soon to talk about that stuff—I don't have names for anything yet. I'm still talking with just Vijaya right now.

Spurgeon: Was it always a foregone conclusion that there would be a next project? Are you used to working on a new project—do you like having something new on the plate?

Smith: I think as long as I have something to do, I'll want to do it. You just made me think of something. When I began *RASL* I did it with this idea that I did *Bone* at pretty much five issues a year. I was regular, even though my reputation was *not* that. [*laughs*] I worked really hard, and I got *Bone* out. I thought with *RASL*, instead of killing myself and doing a book every two months, I'd do a book every four months and it'd be fine. How often does [Dan] Clowes put out a book? Or [Chris] Ware? But boy, that was not met with much sympathy at all. Readers got mad, and retailers . . . so I tried to step it up. I would love to coast a little bit, but it might not be possible.

Spurgeon: You've always been supportive of the Comic Book Legal Defense Fund. It's their anniversary this year as well. While you haven't gone to an obscenity trial with *Bone*, you have been hassled for the not all-the-way G-rated, not 1970s Disney version of fantasy that gets portrayed in that work. Do you have any reflection on the Fund's anniversary? Do you think your fellow creators are still behind what they do over there?

Smith: Yeah. I think it's actually grown. For a long time, Marvel and DC wouldn't have anything to do with it. Then DC jumped in. I think it's important. As you just mentioned: *Bone*, for god's sake, is under attack. Good Christ. If *Bone* can be under attack . . . and it *is* one of the most contested books in school right now. We have to have some way of standing up to people that think they can control others' freedom of speech; that can tell a medium what to do.

Spurgeon: When you arrived, and started to become a bigger name, it seemed like the free speech issues were part of many issues. Even the act of self-publishing had a political element to it.

Smith: Ah, remember those days? [*laughter*]

Spurgeon: It doesn't seem like you have that kind of focused attention on a range of issues. Certainly I think you're right that the support for the Fund has broadened, but it sometimes seems like it's the only set of issues with which people engage. Do you think that's a generational thing? Are is it that the options for creators are pretty good right now?

Smith: Keep going, keep going. [*laughs*]

Spurgeon: Do you ever want to sit down with the young people and tell them why these things are important?

Smith: [*laughs*] "Sit down, children, and let me tell you about the olden days." [*laughter*]

Spurgeon: "Uncle Jeff's Indy Comics Tales."

Smith: You raise some good points. I think some of the issues *were* settled. What were our issues? I think we were trying to get shelf space. We were trying to get equal time in the critical press—Fantagraphics rose to that. We were trying to change the model, the business model of comics. Instead of just being pamphlets, we wanted graphic novels accepted by the retail market. And it was eventually. We wanted to get out of the comic stores and get out into the real world, the big box stores. We did that. We won a lot of those battles.

I still go to shows, because I love talking to cartoonists who are right on that edge where I used to be. I still am, maybe not financially anymore, but artistically you never feel like you're secure. I still go to SPX and MoCCA—not every year, but I love talking to those guys. And what I see is they have a different set of problems. They feel secure in their art. There's no question that they can draw a story about whatever they want. And they don't apologize for it. [*laughs*] They do everything. But the marketplace is weird. They moved away from where we were, which was based in the comic book store, to the web. They have communion on the web. I say "they" because I feel a little old and out of touch. You know what I'm saying?

Spurgeon: I do. And if I made you feel old and out of touch, then my mission here is accomplished. [*Smith laughs*]
Smith: Hey, I *like* being a veteran that survived. That's a fine place to be!

Spurgeon: It's just that you were in that last burst of great cartoonists that essentially transformed the industry underneath you, or at least created more options—it made me wonder what you thought there was left to do.
Smith: I do think there's work to do. It's figuring out how the cartoonists will make money through web distribution, through the Internet. Right now there's just not that much money. There's just not a lot of money in having an app and selling a comic that way. It's not going to pay your rent. It might help with the grocery bill, but it's not significant enough. There is a problem to be solved. I'm in it, too. Vijaya and I are trying to figure it out right now, just like everybody else. Marvel, DC, Dark Horse, Fantagraphics—nobody has this figured out. We're right there. It's exciting. I don't think it's solved. The young people . . . listen to me! "The young people." Let's stop this. [*laughter*]

Spurgeon: You mentioned Vijaya again . . . I was going to interview you and Vijaya at San Diego last summer, but I wasn't able to make it out there. We've talked about this before, but I think Vijaya's contributions are underappreciated. Is there something you feel she's added to the landscape that you wished more people recognized?
Smith: When I talk to people, I know they recognize what she's done.

Spurgeon: Oh, sure.

Smith: She's my partner. I get a lot of credit for making smart moves in the industry. She made those decisions with me. A lot of them were led by her, like making sure our rights were intact so we could use them again on the next thing. She's written a lot of contracts that have gone on to be used by other people in the industry. Anything anyone gives me credit for, they should give credit to her, too.

Comic Relief with Jeff Smith of *RASL* and *Bone*

SEAN EDGAR / 2012

Paste Magazine (August 10, 2012). Reprinted with permission.

In Comic Relief, *Paste* chats with some of the most influential writers and artists in sequential art to discuss the work that inspired them as well as their own contributions. This week features indie icon Jeff Smith, the writer and artist behind the epic *Bone* saga and hardboiled sci-fi thriller *RASL,* which concluded earlier this month.

In early 2008, Smith pivoted from the whimsical, high-fantasy tone he'd established in his fifty-five-issue *Bone* title to focus on an alcoholic, womanizing scientist named Rob who also happens to steal art from parallel dimensions. The wildly inventive, high concept *RASL* spun such influences as *noir,* sci-fi and south-west spiritualism into an addictive chronicle of science gone bad on a colossal scale. With final issue #15 out, Smith was happy to discuss his influences and approach for plotting his sprawling tale of a modern Icarus. He was also kind enough to lay a few hints about his next humorous project and give updates on the movie adaptations of *Bone,* currently tied to *Peter Pan* director P. J. Hogan, and *RASL,* which was optioned by *Harry Potter* and *Sherlock Holmes* producer Lionel Wigram last year. A massive Spoiler Alert for those who are currently reading or plan to read any of Smith's work.

FIRST COMIC WRITTEN

Jeff Smith: It was the first issue of *Bone.*

Sean Edgar: Would your work on the *Thorn* strip you created for Ohio State's student newspaper *The Lantern* count?

Smith: Well, I suppose it would. It was a test run on *Bone.* It had the same characters and setting, but it didn't have a story. It was more just silly, slapstick fish-out-of-water stuff. Here are these crazy Bones who come from somewhere where they used to have computers and telephones, and now they're stuck in a medieval fairy tale forest.

FIRST COMIC READ

Smith: Boy, that's a good question. It was probably an *Uncle Scrooge* comic.

Edgar: Was it one of Carl Barks's?
Smith: Oh sure, those were the ones that really got me.

Edgar: I wonder if he still tours around all of the comic cons doing sketches like he used to.
Smith: You're thinking of Don Rosa, the artist who was his successor.

Edgar: You're absolutely right.
Smith: Carl Barks was alive in the nineties, and he might have done tours, but it was really Don Rosa, heir apparent, who used to come to Mid-Ohio Con all the time. In fact, Don Rosa still sends me chili peppers. He grows crazy, crazy chili peppers in his garden and sends me boxes of them every now and then. They're fantastic.

FAVORITE COMIC OF ALL TIME

Smith: I'm going to have to say *Thimble Theatre Starring Popeye* by E. C. Segar. That's a comic strip, and probably the gold standard. There's also *Krazy Kat* and *Pogo*. For favorite comic book, when I was a kid Joe Kubert did a run on *Tarzan* that just knocked my socks off. I still look at it sometimes. It's an amazing thing.

FAVORITE CURRENT COMIC FROM A PUBLISHER YOU DON'T CURRENTLY WORK FOR

Smith: Which is pretty much all of them (*laughs*). Well, recently I've read a lot of small press comics, and probably have four that I could run off the top of my head. One was *Goliath* by Tom Gauld. Another was *Hark! A Vagrant* by Kate Beaton. *Daytripper* by Fabio Moon and Gabriel Ba. And *Jerusalem* by Guy Delisle. That's the kind of stuff I'm into now.

FAVORITE COMIC BOOK MOVIE

Smith: I'm gonna roll old school and say it was the first *Superman* movie, the 1978 one. That still holds up, man. That's a gorgeous film.

CRAZIEST FAN STORY

Smith: (*Laughs*) Oh my, I have so many. Yeah, I'm just going to pass on that. I can't say that out loud.

Edgar: Is there a truncated, PC version?
Smith: Well, there was a woman who got me to draw a Ted the Bug for her. She was going to tattoo it. And then she came and saw me at another signing, and there were hundreds of people there lined up to get their *Bone* books signed. She waited in line, and she got up to me and asked, "You want to see the tattoo?" I said, "Yeah," and she started to take her pants off, and we all went, "WAIT! WAIT! WAIT!" (*Laughs*) There were all these kids there. We all laughed really hard.

Edgar: That seems fairly good-natured if a little unorthodox.
Smith: Yeah, I can't think of a dangerous one off the top of my head.

Edgar: You've just completed your second epic with the conclusion of *RASL*. How's it feel?
Smith: Oh, it feels great. It was a very fun project to work on. I was completely absorbed for the entire four and a half years I was working on it, and I feel pretty good about the ending. It came together. Sometimes that's not so obvious.

Edgar: *RASL* launched in early 2008. You'd release *Little Mouse Gets Ready* a year later for TOON Books, and Scholastic, arguably the largest book distributor for schools, had been publishing *Bone* in color since 2005. Was there any pressure to keep your work all ages before you published *RASL*?
Smith: That's a good question. When I first started talking about *RASL*, which was like in 2000, I was still in the middle of doing *Bone*, and in 2000, *Bone* was not considered a children's book. It was still being done for the indie, underground market of direct comic book stores. So when I first started playing with the idea of doing a hardboiled story with a sci-fi twist, I wasn't considered a children's author at that time. It came together as it was; it was a story I

wanted to tell. And in 2008 when I really started *RASL* in earnest, *Bone* was by then a bona fide children's book. And I was aware that the audience would be different, but I couldn't worry about it. That was the story I wanted to work on and I just leapt into it.

Edgar: Geography and places tend to be giant influences on your work. You'd included Ohio locales like Old Man's Cave and Athens in *Bone,* and you had said that Arizona was your muse for *RASL.* What about these places and the desert inspire your stories?

Smith: Well, with *Bone* I spent so much time as a kid growing up in Old Man's Cave, which is a real state park about forty miles south of Columbus. It's a real place. It's beautiful and has a giant, gorgeous overhang that was clearly lived in year-round by Indians 150 years ago. Being there really fired my imagination. So when I tried to build a fantasy forest for my Bones to stumble into, that was my setting for it. With *RASL,* I've always been drawn to the American Southwest. I'd been there a few times as a teenager and then I would go back occasionally on my own. It just fit the idea of a noir story. Noir is about man pitted against himself. What better place to put him than in a desert where he's alone and isolated? I was reading the comics webpage *Bleeding Cool* and it described *RASL* as a little desert drive-in movie. And I think that's about right. It's a little potboiler with a sci-fi twist. I include lots of other things to keep everybody interested, like Tesla and conspiracy theories and physics philosophy, my usual meanderings.

Edgar: The Columbus bar references were a nice touch too.

Smith: Are you living through the electric storm, too? (Columbus was experiencing a thunderstorm at the time of the interview)

Edgar: Yes!

Smith: Nice to be talking about *RASL* while the lightning is crackling around us.

Edgar: Tesla and the *noir* genre are the other most recognizable components, along with some Native American mythology. How did all of your research, so much of it that you included a bibliography in your most recent collection, come about? Did the story come first or vice versa?

Smith: Usually there's a spark of an idea. Something that I wanted. And I had the idea first for the character. He had these warp engines that would allow him to go back and forth between parallel dimensions, then I began searching around for context. The original idea was what if you could go into a parallel world and see what your life could have been like. You could meet your girlfriend in the parallel world, but you'd actually have never met and she's married to somebody else. That kind of idea. As that bubbled around, I began to think what kind of story it is. I did the same thing with *Bone*. And I was watching *The Maltese Falcon* and *The Big Sleep*, reading Dashiell Hammett stories, so it all came together. I'm a stickler for science in science fiction stories to be hard. I want it to be based on something real. I just started doing a lot of research in many different directions. I spent time in the Sonoran Desert in Arizona, I read books; I watched *Nova* DVDs to get all of my string theory correct. I think that's the best time, before you've actually started the project and you've just got an idea. You have research you want to do and you play around with ideas.

Edgar: The scenes of multiple realities folding in on themselves were particularly horrific. How did you come up with the initial imagery?
Smith: That was cued off by the Philadelphia Experiment. If you're an *X-Files* fan or conspiracy nut, that's the story of the destroyer escort in World War II that the government wrapped with magnetic cables and ran power through. They not only wanted to make the ship invisible to radar, but they actually wanted to bend light around it and make it invisible. It flashed in and out and disappeared and reappeared like three hundred miles away. There are many variations of the story. But the conclusion is when the ship reappeared, the crew was half embedded in the bulkhead. I jumped from there: if you had a big enough magnet, you might open up the pressure between two universes and have a really bad version of that.

Edgar: I had never seen anything so creatively disturbing.
Smith: Why thank you (*laughs*). I throw out a lot of disturbing, spooky stuff in *Bone* as well, but because they're little cartoon characters I've gotten away with it.

Edgar: The locusts were pretty terrifying. Speaking of spooky, villain Sal Crow opens up a philosophical element at the end of the book. His claims that "Ours is the only universe" and "Man was created to dominate nature" could definitely apply to more than a few issues today, but stretch back to the Galileo trials.
Smith: Well, that was the idea. I had to look at how a noir story is constructed. You usually have the hard luck hero, the femme fatale, and there's usually another dangerous character in the mix. And you have a triangle there. And as I

worked on these characters and constructed them, Maya became the femme fatale. Of course, she was not seen through most of the book, but she was pulling the strings. And Sal became the violent troublemaker. As I worked on everybody's motivations, Maya had to have a reason for doing what she does, Rob/RASL had his motivations and Sal had his motivations. First of all, he was assigned to the case to get RASL. But I wanted it to be more personal, so it just kind of worked out that way. He not only wanted to stop RASL from doing what he was doing, but he wanted to completely destroy what RASL had found because it offended him.

Edgar: It's all the more ironic when Sal, a religious character, is ultimately stopped by the little girl referred to as "God."
Smith: (*Laughs*) Ironic.

Edgar: On the topic of that little girl, everything wrapped up nicely but she is left with quite a bit of mystery. Is there a backstory to her or are you leaving that one alone?
Smith: I think that one can just hang there. I don't think RASL quite knows what she is, but he knows that she's just not a little girl. He knows that she's from the multiverse and was able to follow him. I'm quite content to let people puzzle over that and have fun with it.

Edgar: Do you have an origin story for her locked inside your head?
Smith: Yes, I know who she is. I know where she came from.

Edgar: Of course the ending was classic noir. Femme fatale Maya's deception was planted from the first issue and you laid a lot of clues.
Smith: Does that mean you actually went back and read?

Edgar: Absolutely.
Smith: Excellent.

Edgar: Were there any readers who popped up mid-story and said, "I know it's all Maya and Uma!"
Smith: Not one. I couldn't believe it. Not one. I even labeled the third trade book *Romance at the Speed of Light,* and no one suggested, "Hey, is that what RASL's name means?" I was surprised, because there were some people who guessed some of the surprises ahead of time. With RASL, I slipped through.

Edgar: It's traditional *noir,* with the femme fatale emerging as puppet master.
Smith: And then at the end, she confesses everything in three paragraphs. I thought that was really fun. (*Laughs*)

Edgar: Rob left the series riding off into the sunset. Do you think you'll ever return to the *RASL* universe?
Smith: I'm not really a sequel guy, but *RASL* is wide open for one. It sure feels like there's another adventure there. For one thing, Rob's and Sal's teleportation suits are laying somewhere on their real earths' deserts, somewhere. They just left them there. Somebody could find those. So yeah, there's potential.

Edgar: Moving onward, I had heard rumors of a space book discussed some years ago at the end of *Bone.* Is that another project, or did that turn into *RASL?*
Smith: I'd been talking about *RASL* since 2000, and at one point I was talking with Paul Pope about the two of us doing a giant book, and half of it would be *RASL* and the other half would be a story that he did. And then our schedules never worked out and I just ended up doing *RASL.*

Edgar: So do you have any concrete ideas for your next project?
Smith: I do. I'm working on it right now. I have some props on my desk that are staring at me getting ready. But I'm going to be mum about it before I get a little bit more to show.

Edgar: Can I pry out any details at all?
Smith: I'm not ready to say the title or anything, but I think it will be humor. It'll be closer to *Bone* than it is to *RASL.*

Edgar: Is there any current news on the *Bone* movie from Warner Bros.? Last we heard Patrick Sean Smith, P. J. Hogan, and animation studio Animal Logic were looking at early 2013 for the first film. Any updates?
Smith: I like everybody involved. They're all working very hard on it, but it's becoming apparent to me that I write comics that are just incredibly hard to adapt into movies. So I don't know. They're still rewriting the scripts and it's still in motion. They're still trying to make it happen.

Edgar: Is there a window for when the movie might be released?
Smith: No. No window.

Edgar: Are you happy with what you've seen?

Smith: Everything I've seen I've thought was very good. I like the director (P. J. Hogan) on a personal level, and I think his movies are very interesting and good. I'm just waiting for the studio to say they're happy with the script and get it going. I know Animal Logic is chomping at the bit to get started.

Edgar: Is there any news on bringing *RASL* to the big screen?

Smith: Oh yeah. Wigram Productions picked up the option last year. They're at Warner Bros. also. They're the guys who did the big *Sherlock Holmes* movies with Robert Downey Jr., and they're working like hell on it. I just got a new *RASL* script this weekend as a matter of fact, so I just read it and I know this weekend another *Bone* script is going to drop. So like I said, everybody's working really hard on it. Just got to get the stars to line up.

Edgar: In a perfect world, who would play RASL?

Smith: Oh, man. Every now and then I'll see an actor, and a young Charles Bronson is just like RASL. What do I know? Half the time I was picturing Brad Pitt, the other half of the time I was picturing Matt Damon. But I don't really think about that too much.

"We Don't Have to Be That Political Anymore": An Interview with Jeff Smith

CHRIS MAUTNER / 2013

The Comics Journal (November 4, 2013). Reprinted with permission.

Pity the artist who has to follow up a mega-successful, critically acclaimed, game-changing work. Sure, having achieved such incredible success in the first place mitigates any desire to throw a pity party, but it's an unenviable task all the same.

If Jeff Smith felt any pressure putting together a follow-up to the phenomenon known as *Bone*, he doesn't let it show. While *RASL*, his *noir*-tinged, sci-fi saga differs in tone and content from *Bone,* the change stems from an artist following his own interests, as Smith notes below, rather than from any direct and deliberate attempt to shift away from what he's best known for.

After being serialized over the past few years in a number of different formats, *RASL* is now available in a chunky hardcover edition, in full color to boot. Smith said he considers this the definitive edition of the work, and the subdued, muted palette does give the comic an added vibrancy. Certainly Smith's gritty, trippy story of parallel universes, metaphysics, government conspiracies, and vast Arizona vistas serves as a reminder of what a consummate and considered cartoonist he is.

I cornered Smith at this year's Small Press Expo in Bethesda, Md., almost immediately after his Q&A panel. We found a quiet spot on the lower level and while my daughter read comics, I peppered Smith with questions about *RASL* and comics culture in general.

Chris Mautner: What was the last SPX you attended?

Jeff Smith: The last one was 2008. So it's been about four years since I've been here. I went to the first SPX and I went to all of them from whenever they started in 1994 or so to about 2001 or 2002. Back then we used to have a one-day show on Saturday, and on Sunday we'd have a pig roast and we'd play softball against Diamond. It was much smaller. It was a crazier event in some ways.

Mautner: Looking around at the show today, how has SPX changed, and how is that change emblematic of what's happened in comics in general?

Smith: Well, my goodness. My first reaction when I came through the lobby last night was, "Oh my god, look at all these people I don't know!" And they're all 12! They're obviously not 12, but to someone my age, anyone in their twenties looks so fresh-faced.

One of the biggest differences is for so many of these people it just doesn't even occur to them that they shouldn't do comics. It's a totally normal career choice: "I'm going to make comics." For boys and girls. It's so different in tone, and the energy level is off the hook. I'm excited by it. I'm wound up by it.

Mautner: To what extent was *RASL* a conscious shift away for you from *Bone* and its success? How much of it consisted of you being interested in *noir* and sci-fi and how much of it was you wanting to do something markedly different from *Bone* in tone?

Smith: It was not a conscious decision at all to move away from *Bone*. As I was explaining on the panel just now, when I first came up with the concept for *RASL,* it was four years before I finished *Bone*. In 2000, *Bone* was not a children's book yet. I was just thinking, "I did this comedy-adventure book and now I'm going to do a more hardcore sci-fi book." It didn't even occur to me that the audiences would be different. But the audiences have changed so drastically in the last fifteen years. The reality was that when I finally did *RASL* there were kids reading comics again and *Bone* was considered a children's book. By that point I had to deal with the fact that the audience was going to have different expectations from me. But it was too late! It was the story I wanted to do and I'm doing it [*laughs*].

I just don't think that it's that different a story. I get that it is, and I see how people think it is, but for me it didn't change my thinking that much. For me, it was exciting to try to learn the tropes of a different kind of story. And it was hard to get out from under *Bone's* shadow. I spent so much time on [*Bone*]. It was a little break.

Mautner: So in that sense did *RASL* afford you a chance to shift your focus?

Smith: Maybe that is what it was. I think I was hopeful I would be able to do something again. It was enjoyable for me to do something that wasn't the same thing I had been doing for twelve years. Does that make sense?

Mautner: That makes a lot of sense. You were talking [in the panel] about how you were doing more horizontal panels [for *RASL*]. Other than that, were there any other deliberate stylistic ways you tried to make *RASL* different from *Bone?*
Smith: There are a couple. The one you just mentioned was to deliberately do a different kind of panel layout, one I thought would be more appropriate for this kind of story. I don't know exactly why, except that I was doing a different kind of action, and I thought [more horizontal panels] would speed things up and also pull each image out a little further in your peripheral vision.

There are these little moments of meditation on Nikola Tesla that are very different than anything I did in *Bone.* They're not flashbacks per se but *RASL's* interior workings. It's him working through his memories of Tesla's story. It's a very different style. I didn't treat Tesla as a character in the book. You don't see him walking around his lab talking to people. I treated it more like a documentary. My Italian publisher hit the nail on the head when he said, "What you're doing with the Tesla meditations, it's where Herman Melville writes about the whale's head for no reason for five pages."

Mautner: One thing I noticed that's different is that *Bone* is pretty much a straightforward narrative from beginning to end, and in *RASL* you're jumping around in time a lot. There are a lot more flashbacks, there's a lot more work for the reader in terms of keeping track—not just of the characters—but of where we are in the story. Can you talk a little about that?
Smith: It was because the nature of the story was parallel universes and also *noir*, which has a lot of history of mazes. The maze of the city. The maze of the lies you've woven around yourself. So I thought it tied in stylistically with the concept of him being lost in a maze and parallel universes to keep the reader a little disoriented, especially at first. I never said what city they were in. I wanted you to feel a little disoriented or at least not know exactly where you were and what was going on. And then slowly I stared letting you know they're in Tucson and the Sonoran Desert.

The other reason was hard-boiled stories are [told in] first person. Which is very different from what I did in *Bone. Bone* was a straightforward adventure story where you could go from what Phone Bone and Thorn were doing over to what Smiley Bone and Phoney Bone were up to. Or you could jump to the bad guys up in the mountains. You could hear them plotting and figure out what they're doing. Whereas in this kind of a hard-boiled story, you only know what the protagonist knows.

Mautner: And that makes for a more insular story.
Smith: It creates a very claustrophobic situation for the reader and for the writer as well. It was a little hard cause you have to figure out how he's going to find out everything you need the reader to know. You really find yourself twisted up in knots sometimes.

Mautner: You've talked a lot about how your interest in *noir* and sci-fi led to *RASL*, but there are also themes of mythology, religion, and faith that run through the book. There's the lizard-faced villain that's coming from a specific religious perspective, for example. And the Southwestern Native American mythology seems to be a strong motif.
Smith: There were similar themes in *Bone* as well. It's what interests me in writing: Exploring things you can't see or the life forces that surround us and interact with us. With *RASL*, the parallel universes obviously suggest that we cannot see everything. That opened up the whole idea where I could start talking about the symbolism used by the Indians of the Southwest, which I was able to overlap with the maze idea. The American Indians of the Southwest, all these different cultures and tribes, they all used this man in the maze concept. I just took that maze concept and introduced it into the story. The maze itself stands for *Follow the maze* and every time you reach a turning point, it's like a life choice or life event has passed, and the closer you get to the center, the faster and faster the turning points come. It all just overlaps so perfectly with [RASL's] maze of parallel universes and bad life choices.

Mautner: You said early on, when the first issue came out, how you wanted to create a character that made bad choices and was almost unlikeable. Did that change? Did your initial conception of the book alter?
Smith: In some ways it has to. When you serialize a book—and I always write the ending, so the ending is the same ending that I always intended. Some of the major plot points were always going to happen. Thing present themselves—I can't think of an example off the top of my head, but I did it with *Bone* as well, where an opportunity or something interesting pops up and I follow it. And I just try to keep it under control so it fits in with the story and I can get [the characters] back [to where they need to be]. There's a moment at the end of *RASL* where there's a bunch of birds falling out of the sky. It's a

huge, mass bird die-off. I only learned in the middle of writing the book that it was tied into conspiracy theories about the antennae ray and Tesla, which my fictional St. George Ray is based on. And so if I learn those things I can add them into the story. You have to be quick on your feet.

Mautner: So were you researching the whole time you were working on the book?
Smith: Constantly. It did grow. The personal stories got a little bigger. I don't think I had originally fleshed out the relationship between RASL and his partner that much but once the Nikola Tesla thing really kicked in and became part of the book it became something for those two characters to share and have a past about it. And that opened up different things to write about.

Mautner: Why did you decide to set this in the Southwest? Because usually when you think of noir, you think of Southern California or urban areas. Or when you think of sci-fi you think of futuristic cities and other worlds. But *RASL* is set in a very specific and different place and time.
Smith: I think my idea was that when you boil down noir what the most important thing was a man against himself. His decisions or his choices he had to make to save himself. He had to survive and it's a really primitive situation. That's how I boiled it down. I thought putting it in the desert would be the perfect place for that, because once you're in the desert there's no one to help you. Symbolically, that's him against nature, against himself, and it enables him to figure out a way out of [things].

Mautner: And it enables you to tie in not just the Native American mythology, but also things like Area 51 and government conspiracies . . .
Smith: Yeah, Raytheon is out in Tucson. Plus, those cacti are in our psyches. We know that stuff. That means the old west. Mano a mano. And that's the kind of tale I'm telling. Which is very different than *Bone*.

Mautner: I wanted to ask about the coloring in *RASL*. I think you initially planned to have this in color?
Smith: Maybe I did. I could have. I went back and forth on it. It was a decision that had to be made at some point. I thought it worked pretty well in black and white; it's a *noir, Maltese Falcon* story. Black and white would have been fine. Steve Hamaker, who colored it with me, we thought if we could find a palette that really worked, that didn't just color it for the sake of it but actually gave the story more power and made the world a little more [real]—I was

definitely interested in doing that. There were things about *RASL* I couldn't really communicate in black and white and that was some of the reflected light and some of the crazy light things you can do with color that I thought would be better. I mean, you can do a lot with black and white. Look at Will Eisner. But there were light things I wanted to do with color and Steve found it. He found some textures and a palette that I thought ended up being very rich and dark and smoky. It works for me. It isn't just a color version. This is the definitive version. I actually like this better than the black and white.

Mautner: Smokey is a good adjective. It has a subdued feel to it.
Smith: And let me tell you, getting that to work on this toothy pulpy paper we picked was crazy difficult. We were working with our printer in Singapore and they were not able to communicate to us what the dot gain on this grade of paper was and we were really sweating it. We went panel by panel making educated guesses on it, we're doing math to figure out how much magenta or cyan to put under the black or, "That's a guy we might need to lighten that up by thirty percent." Crazy things. We were just guessing! I definitely had some sleepless nights waiting for this book to come back from the printer.

Mautner: When you started *RASL* you had a couple different publishing things going. You had the pamphlet, you had the oversized collections and you had the pocket collections. Why so many different versions? What worked, what didn't work, and what did you take away from that experience?
Smith: The reason we did more than one version, quite honestly, is that *RASL* didn't get a lot of traction after the initial burst of publicity that "The *Bone* guy is going to do something new!" It was not really taking, I could tell. So we got the first oversized trade out, that was the size I wanted to do it in, but again, I didn't really feel like it was getting traction. I didn't hear it being talked about or hardly even being reviewed.

This is one of the advantages of being a self-publisher: You can move fast on your feet. You don't have to give up. I don't have to ask anyone's permission to fix it. So we thought maybe that first trade has 115 pages in it but it might not be enough of the story. Maybe we should have waited until we had a little more story. So that's why we did the pocket book version, which was—it wasn't the size we were interested in. We wanted to get two of the larger books, so we'd have double the story and see if that would catch people's attention. And that in fact did work. We started seeing reviews and began to get a bit of traction.

Mautner: I was going to ask you how you felt *RASL* has been received because it did seem to me that it was getting lost in the mix and I wondered if part of that was that we are in an age where people are waiting for the [completed] book.

Smith: That's probably true, and I'm as much to blame as anybody for that. [*laughter*] The sales were decent on it as a serialized book. It started off close to twenty thousand and ended up in the twelve thousand range, which is enough to justify its existence. I think you can tell by the love that my team at Cartoon Books has poured into this that we hope that this is the version that will attract attention. I don't want to sound negative. It was getting good reviews from fairly outstanding places like *Publishers Weekly* and newspapers. We were getting really good reviews the whole time, starred reviews from Booklist. So it was getting good critical reviews the comic book world just wasn't . . . lighting on fire about it.

Mautner: Right. Like they did with *Bone*. Of course, nothing's ever going to do that.

Mautner: Comics culture has become rather balkanized in recent years and there's little overlap between the different markets—the SPX people don't mix with the manga people, etc. I wonder if that makes it harder for certain authors to get their work out there and get attention.

Smith: It might, but I don't think that's the case with me. It's always been stratified, somewhat artificially. Remember, when we were kids, if you liked Marvel you weren't allowed to like DC. There were all these demarcations and lines in the sand that have always been there. If you like superhero comics you don't like the non-superhero comics. Even today, in our little pocket of indie comics there are stratifications of "These are art comics and these are indie comics." And all of that is completely made up. It makes no difference. If Dan Clowes is a brilliant cartoonist, just because of the subject matter, that shouldn't put him into a certain strata. It's because of his skills. It's because of his chops.

Mautner: Talking about format and style, I wanted to ask about your next project, *Tuki Saves the Humans*. You said you're serializing this online. What led to your decision to do that? Are you down on the pamphlet now?

Smith: No, I'm not down on the pamphlet, and I don't think print is going away, but clearly the future is digital. There's no way you can ignore it. I haven't seen a good model for making money online. It seems like the webcartoonists that have succeeded and are making money have somehow transitioned into the book distribution world that's more traditional way of making money. Someone like Kate Beaton. She's a webcomics artist but she's making money now because she has a book and that book is going through normal channels. Faith Erin Hicks has also done a similar thing. I think that's a good model. It seems to be working. And I just decided I want to try it. Again, I'm a self-publisher. I can experiment. And if it doesn't work, you'll see me turn around and try something else very quickly.

Mautner: Can you summarize the story?

Smith: It's going to be a Pleistocene-era story that takes place two million years ago when there was one of the first big ice ages. This is the one that locked all the moisture up in one of the polar ice caps. Africa is dry as a bone and all the creatures that live there, including early hominids, and all the animals, they were losing their jungle environments and were becoming extinct, including early man. At some point someone was the first one to leave Africa. There was someone who left Africa and populated the rest of the world. I want to tell that guy's story. All the forces of Africa, the other humans, the animals and ancient gods are going to do their best to stop him.

And I have the ending written. I always write the ending before I make that first page.

Mautner: Comics culture has changed so much since you started *Bone*, and *Bone* has played such a large part in that change. I feel like you have a unique perspective because you straddle so many spheres. You're a comics guy, you're someone who started in the traditional comics format, but you've been published by a book publisher, you've got a young adult fan base, etc. When you look at the comics industry as a whole, do you see it as healthy? What's your take on where we stand?

Smith: I would have to say it looks pretty healthy. Especially [compared to] twenty years ago, when there were so many rules and conventionally wrong ideas about comics. First of all there were no kids reading comics. Your daughter is sitting here reading a comic right in front of us. And she's making comics. That is healthy for us as lovers of comics, as creators of comics, as writers about comics. It couldn't be better.

I remember very clearly the day in the late nineties when I noticed it wasn't just guys in their thirties on the showroom floors. All of the sudden I began to see young couples, young girlfriends—two girlfriends holding hands and going, "I'm going to go shopping for comics." I'm like, "What's happening?" This is a wonderful, wonderful thing.

There were periods where early in the mid-nineties when declarations were being made that children were lost to comics. They're not going to read at all, they're going to play video games and watch movies and TV. Between manga and the Scholastic books there are [now] millions of kids who want to read comics. And there's the fact that we were able to get out of the comic book store ghetto. I love comic book stores and they still represent a large part of my audience, but we needed to be out of there.

We used to talk about comics all night, every night, all of us of that generation. All we wanted to do was get our comics read by the widest possible audience. And one of the problems, especially for those of us starting to think of this long-form format, where we were going to serialize very long stories with a literary structure and a beginning, middle and end—the problem was comics were sold like magazines. They were up on the shelf for four weeks and when the new issue came out that one went down and into a long box never to be seen again, except by a collector. Someone like me, who is writing a story that's planned out as a 1,400-page novel—I need people to be able to read that first chapter.

In the back of *Wizard* it said *Bone* #1 was worth three hundred dollars. Nobody can read it! So we had to get political about the whole thing. We would have pizza parties or meetings at Dave Sim's penthouse suite back in the day and we'd meet with retailers, especially key retailers that were on our side and believed in us, and say, "You've got to stock graphic novels." Once you sell out, buy them again! It's like if you have a hardware store and you sell out of hammers, you get more hammers! We would explain to them, these are profit centers. You can count on these.

We had other prejudices we had to get over. Self-publishing—only in comics was it a badge of honor. Outside of comics, there were guidelines. Baker & Taylor wouldn't touch a comic and they wouldn't touch self-publishing. So we had all these battles.

Mautner: Do you feel like those battles have been won?

Smith: Yes and no. From an actual standpoint where we were trying to get more shelf space in the stores and into [other] distribution systems into libraries and big box stores. Those were very much our goals: Wider audiences for small press, the work of an author with a voice.

In that sense, yeah, I think we did win. Because there were battles just to get out of Artist's Alley. This show we're at right now came out of a conversation between Dave Sim and I, where we were like, "Let's go on the road"—cause we were like two kings for a couple of years. "Let's go on the road," and we contacted a bunch of good stores all around the country and . . . the next year [we visited] the Bethesda store. But then they started SPX and we were there.

We needed to control it cause the system that was in place was not there for us in terms of San Diego, the conventions, the stores, certainly not Barnes & Noble. So yes, in that manner, we checked [these things] off [our list] and we live in that world now. We don't have to be that political anymore.

Still, in terms of outreach, I still meet occasional librarians that are like, "This isn't reading. I understand why kids like graphic novels because they can do other things while they're reading it." What? [*laughter*] It'll never be done. But that's the new generation's problem. Let these young Turks handle it. I'm old and tired.

The World of Comics with *The Best American Comics 2013* Editor Jeff Smith

DAVID HARPER / 2013

Multiversity Comics (November 25, 2013). Reprinted with permission.

Every year, Houghton Mifflin Harcourt releases a new edition of *The Best American Comics*, each time with a different guest editor picking their favorite comic releases of the year. This year? None other than *Bone* creator Jeff Smith edits the book and highlights the work of brilliant creators like Alison Bechdel, Kate Beaton, Evan Dorkin, Jill Thompson, Terry Moore and many, many more.

Today, we talked to Smith about this release, what it made him think about today's crops of comics and creators, recapturing the excitement of your youth through comics, his new webcomic (which has now started!), titled *Tuki Save the Humans*, and even what's next for the world of *Bone*. Thanks to Harcourt for the opportunity to talk with Smith (who is one of my all-time favorite creators). Very exciting to chat with him, unsurprisingly.

David Harper: You were given the chance to be the editor for the 2013 edition of *The Best American Comics*, and I have to say, it's one of my favorite editions yet. For you, what appealed to you the most about putting together this collection, and as someone who just loves the medium, how exciting was it to just get in deep with all of the magic happening in comics today?

Jeff Smith: It was very cool. I've always loved going to small press shows to see what newer cartoonists are up to, and this was like that in spades! I was in deep!

Harper: One of my favorite things in the book was in your intro where you stated that there was one day when preparing for this endeavor that all you did was sit with a plate of cookies and milk and read comics. It was an awesome little anecdote. As a reader, do some comics appeal to you on a sheerly trans-portive level, taking you back to your youth? I know that's a feeling I often love having when reading certain comics.

Smith: Of course. Some of my fondest memories as a kid involve comic books. I have a strong memory of riding my bike to the drug store when I was ten to buy candy and comics, and finding the first issue of Joe Kubert's *Tarzan*. The artwork was like nothing I'd ever seen before. Blew a gasket in my brain. I bought the comic—a hefty twenty-five cents, and rode home as fast as I could. I threw my bike down and sat on the porch and read that magazine three times through before I even looked up. I thought it was one of the most perfect things I'd ever seen.

Harper: One of the things your edition of *The Best American Comics* really emphasized to me was just how diverse a medium comics are right now. Was that something you were looking to underline when putting together your choices, or did it just come together naturally?

Smith: I suppose it was unavoidable. Comics are diverse now. There are no rules about what subject matter to use or who your audience must be. What I was looking for were unique voices, cartoonists writing what they wanted to, the way they wanted to as authors. A good comic is a good comic. The collection reflects my tastes. I read Alison Bechdel and Sammy Harkham. I love Evan Dorkin and Kate Beaton. What I want is a comic that works—-that makes me pay attention and even believe in it for the time it's in front of me.

Harper: I love how many incredible female cartoonists were featured in this edition, and you highlighted some of my favorites. As someone who has been in the industry for a while now, how cool is it to see people like Faith Erin Hicks and Kate Beaton bringing such amazing work to life in a medium that long felt like an all-boys club?

Smith: I think it's great. Frankly, they are some of the best comics in the book!

Harper: Speaking of Kate, I have to ask, how bizarre was it to find out the two of you are actually related at SPX?

Smith: Very. At the start of our conversation, we had no idea, then suddenly we realized there was a connection. My dad's family is from a little town in Nova Scotia called Mabou—- I knew Kate was from somewhere near Halifax, so I asked where. When she answered Mabou, I thought I'd impress her with the fact that I knew the place. We had a Smith family reunion there, and we all hung out at the Red Shoe tavern. When I mentioned the Red Shoe, she looked like someone hit her on the head with a hammer! Well, that was it. We started talking and suddenly we realized that both our parents have a copy of the same book, *The Smiths of Cape Breton*. Katie is interested in genealogy and even had a job for a while tracing people's family trees. Turns out the Beatons and the Smiths are related, and we share a great, great, etc. grandfather. The world is suddenly smaller, and my family is a little bigger. It's not the kind of thing that happens every day. Only at SPX!

Harper: What would you say the biggest things you took away from the experience as editor of *The Best American Comics* were?
Smith: Two things. The breadth of talent, and the relative youth of so many cartoonists. Most in their twenties and thirties.

Harper: Given the amount of youth and diversity in this edition, what do you think your year-long experience of pouring through as many comics as you could get your hands taught you about where comics are as a medium today?
Smith: I think we're in a good place. Comics will probably never be an easy place to make a living, but the art form has a lot of respect now, and there are more opportunities than ever to make whatever kind of book you want.

Harper: Webcomics earned a lot of space in the book, and now you have your own webcomic coming in November in *Tuki Save the Humans*. Would you say the experience of seeing what webcomics had to offer partially inspired taking your work to this format, or was that something that had already been on your mind?
Smith: It had an influence. The web looks fresh to me, and the comics I saw there made me want to experiment with layout and more open designs. Not only did I read good stuff online, but people like Kate and Faith Erin Hicks are actually making it pay. Like them, Vijaya and I plan to serialize *Tuki* for free, then eventually release a printed book.

Harper: What can you tell us about *Tuki Save the Humans*, both from a story standpoint and how you intend to play around with the format/layout of your work?
Smith: It takes place 1.8 million years ago when the early hominids were going extinct due to climate changes. In order to survive, something had to be done. *Tuki* tells the story of the first human to leave Africa. It's a comedy adventure in the *Bone* mode, but like *RASL*, it is largely grounded in science. New pages will go up on Mondays, Wednesdays, and Fridays, and each one will be a bit

like a Sunday comics page. The first one will go up Monday, November 25. They can be read for free at boneville.com.

Harper: Out of this year's San Diego Comic Con, word came that you were going to work on new *Bone* stories that'd be entirely from you and not "sequels" but comics that are set in the world of Boneville. What's the road map for that project, and can you tell us anything about that yet?

Smith: I still want to draw the Bone cousins. Not so much do new comics, per se, because the *Bone* story is finished, and I have no desire to revisit the world. I think it would feel like going back to high school, you know what I mean? But the three cousins, that's a different thing. Those boys have been with me my whole life, so Scholastic is working with me to come up with some projects that will give me an excuse to draw them again. But that's all I can say for now. Until then, I hope you'll check out *Tuki* online.

Jeff Smith on Cartoon Books' *Tuki: Save the Humans*

ROGER ASH / 2014

Westfield Comics (Summer 2014). Reprinted with permission.

Jeff Smith is the creator of the popular comics *Bone* and *RASL*. His current story, *Tuki*, is being serialized on his website, Boneville.com. "Tuki Season One" will be available in print this July as *Tuki*: *Save the Humans* #1. Westfield's Roger Ash recently spoke with Smith to learn more about Tuki and his world.

Roger Ash: How did *Tuki* come about?

Jeff Smith: I went to Africa in 1996. Vijaya and I went with Larry Marder and his wife, Larry's the *Beanworld* cartoonist, and while we were there, we were in Tanzania and we visited the Olduvai Gorge which is where the Leakey's did a lot of their excavations. Over millions of years, different species of humans lived there and I remember looking at some of the fossils that they had on display. It's outside, so you're standing there and you can feel the sun coming down on you and smell the plants and the animals and see the dirt and the grass. I remember really being able to picture our ancestors alive and walking around. That was the very beginning of the idea.

Ash: How much research did you do for this?

Smith: I did a lot of research into what order our ancestors came in and tried to figure out at what point they were able to start talking. It's amazing. Experts can look at the base of a Homo erectus skull and see that it had a long enough voice box so it could modulate sound. Also, they can look at impressions inside of the skull and see that it had a Broca's area which is a major speech center. We don't know that two million years ago Homo erectus could talk the way that we do, but they certainly were the first ones who had the equipment.

Ash: Did you also do research into what the landscape would have been like and what animals were around as well?

Smith: Absolutely. I wanted to know what plants were around so when Tuki eats a fruit, he's eating fruit that we think might have been around back then. It's somewhat conjecture, but I went with what the experts think. And, of course, dinosaurs were gone for sixty-three million years when we showed up, so there are no dinosaurs in *Tuki*.

Ash: But there was megafauna around at the time.

Smith: Yes, there were some big animals including the saber tooth, which is my favorite.

Ash: What can you tell us about the story?

Smith: As I was doing the research, I came across a couple of different epochs when a turning point was reached. The one that I settled on that I thought would make a good story was two million years ago for two reasons. One: at that time, there were multiple different human species living at the same time; they were overlapping. So you had Australopithecus, you had Homo habilis, and some Homo erectus. They were all alive at the same time and would have interacted with each other. I thought that was interesting. You don't really think about that very much and it would make a good story.

Also, around that time was one of the world's first ice ages which was changing the world and drying it out in a lot of places and forcing a lot of animals into extinction. But Homo erectus did not go extinct; he left Africa. He dominated the world, in Africa as well, when the other animals went extinct. So it's a turning point where our direct root ancestor took over and survived while all the other human species went extinct. The story doesn't feel like a grand turning point in history. It's just a story of this one guy, Tuki, who is trying to move north. He's walking, just trying to figure out how he can survive the day and get some food. There are people who are against him leaving Africa and they're trying to stop him; mostly ancient spirit gods and things like that.

Ash: Who are some of the other characters we'll meet in the story?

Smith: That's some tricky territory. I don't want to say too much. We've already met a shaman, this Homo habilis character, who is surprising me already. I thought he was going to be a dangerous character, but he immediately turned into a worrying mother type. [*laughter*] I don't know where we're going with him. As soon as "Season Two" starts, which should be the first week of June, we'll meet another Homo erectus; a child. We got a very quick glimpse of him in the last strip I drew. He was way off in the distance and you saw a saber tooth was stalking him. We'll get to meet him. We'll also meet the little ones, we just see their eyeballs in the first season, and those are Australopithecines. That's about all I'll say except that we'll get to meet our first giant.

Ash: You are doing this as a digital comic first. Why did you decide to do that?
Smith: It's obvious that's where we're heading in the future and I wanted to be part of it. That doesn't mean that I think print is going away any time soon, and I certainly don't want it to. Vijaya and I have been doing this for twenty years and when we see a trend, we want to play; we want to get into it and figure it out.

Webcomics are some of my favorite comics right now like *Hark! A Vagrant* by Kate Beaton and *Haunter* by Sam Alden. I just thought it would be fun to do. We are going to do a print version. We're going to do a color comic book that will come out in July, but I was curious about what would happen. Would the ability of people in Europe to read *Tuki* have any effect on the sales? I don't know. We'll find out.

Ash: What sort of challenges did you find telling the story this way as opposed to a twenty-four-page comic?
Smith: One challenge was that the screen was more horizontally shaped, so I had to change my grid and rethink how I look at panels on a page to tell the story. That was fun and I ended up kind of approaching it like the Golden Age of newspaper comics when Hal Foster used to do *Prince Valiant* and Alex Raymond did *Flash Gordon*. They put a lot more emphasis on the illustration. They wanted to leave the audience with something to look at to hold them over until the next week. I thought I'd try that. That also meant the story had to be the same way; I need to do something on every page. It doesn't always have to be a joke, but some thought or process has to be complete on the page. We put them up on Mondays and Fridays and I want to try and evoke that Sunday comic page feeling and give people something to spend time with.

Ash: Are you doing any reformatting for the print version?
Smith: We want to run one strip per page, so that has some challenges. It'll look like a regular comic book on the stand and sit there vertically and have a cover that looks normal. When you pick it up and start to read it, you'll have to turn it and read it horizontally until you get to the end and the letters page and you'll have to flip it back again. We're going to put a little timeline in there too to show people where this took place in the course of time.

Ash: In one of the early strips, you had a note about the monkey orange.

Smith: That's a real fruit that exists today and they think that it has been around for millions of years.

Ash: Are you going to continue putting in little notes like that to point out some of the historical things?

Smith: Yes, I definitely am. I think that's fun. Actually, that's part of what's nice about the webcomic, and I picked that up from reading other people's webcomics, is that little note or interaction with readers which we used to get in comic books through the letters page, but people don't really write letters any longer. [*laughter*] It's all electronic now. But I think that's fun and I think that would be interesting to read in someone else's comic; what research brought them to make that decision. It doesn't really change the strip, but it adds a little interest.

Ash: You mentioned giants and gods, so are there more fantastical elements to the story as well?

Smith: Yeah. I want him to appear like a real human who's hungry and is trying to just survive. I want the surroundings to be very real, but it's very far, far away from us in time. I thought the more research I could do, the more realistic I could make it; the more believable it would be that this was really happening. But at the same time there are non-archeological elements that I could play with which is their superstitions or their beliefs. The shaman was able to create a potion that would allow them to speak to each other. That's fantasy and when the giants start coming into the story, that's not really in the archeological record.

Ash: Is it difficult striking a balance between the two?

Smith: Sure it is. I have to be careful, but that's something I've always found really fun to do. I love to take things that really don't belong together and mash 'em up. So taking something that's historically accurate and putting fantasy into it is right up my alley.

Ash: Reading the strip, I got the impressions that there's definitely some backstory to who Tuki is and why he's leaving Africa. Is that going to be revealed eventually?

Smith: Yes, that would have to be part of the story. You have to figure out a character's backstory before you even start, but sometimes I'm not sure how much of it to actually show. In *Bone*, I had this backstory worked out for

Gran'ma Ben and I just happened to be telling this backstory to my friend Charles Vess, the fantasy painter, and he wanted to draw it. We ended up actually telling the story in *Rose*. I probably never would have told that story; that was just the background in my head that set it up. So we'll see how much of Tuki's backstory comes out.

Five Stars: Starting at the End with Jeff Smith

STEVE MORRIS / 2017

Comics Alliance (March 31, 2017). Reprinted with permission.

There are few cartoonists more admired than Jeff Smith. Inspired himself by the serialized newspaper strips he read as a child, Smith went on to create a string of acclaimed, inspirational comics works that have not only proved evergreen in terms of story but have brought in generation after generation of new excited cartoonists to make their own comics.

Often described as an overnight success, the reality is that Smith worked for years in relative obscurity before self-publishing the series that made his name: *Bone*, the story of three cousins who journey across countless landscapes—sometimes together, often apart—and the various strange and intriguing folk they meet along the way.

As a self-publisher, Smith set up a company called Cartoon Books, originally comprised of just one employee: Jeff Smith. However, over time the rigors of self-publishing meant that his wife Vijaya ultimately left her job to join him—and the company grew in subsequent years to bring in several other staffers, many of whom are still there today.

Bone was published in a serialized format from 1991–2004, with a new story called *Bone: Coda* released in 2016 that put a cap to the series. It marked one of Smith's most notable traits as a storyteller: the need for his works to have a definitive beginning, middle, and end.

Smith always works to make sure he has an ending in place before he starts writing the beginning of each story, with his subsequent self-published stories *RASL* and *Tuki: Save the Humans* both adhering to that rule. As a result, his narratives always have a sense of consistency: he knows where he's heading and every story until that point leads the reader closer to that conclusion.

Following the conclusion of *Bone,* Smith stretched out into more experimental areas: his series *Tuki: Save the Humans* was released as a webcomic before coming to print, and *RASL* was not only aimed at an older readership, but featured a notably different storytelling approach in the art style. Though best known for his self-published work, Smith has also worked on stories for other publishers, partnering with DC for a *Shazam!* miniseries in 2007 as part of a larger project at the publisher, which also brought in Kyle Baker at the same time for a run on *Plastic Man*.

Throughout his career, Smith has proven one thing: careful planning and a considered approach behind the scenes always leads to the most enjoyable storytelling on the page. Having won a number of Eisners in several categories, Smith remains an eclectic, energetic presence within comics —which led him naturally to his current role as the festival director for Comics Crossroads Columbus, which sees the best new and established cartoonists in the world head to the State every year.

Always experimenting, always pushing forward; there's a reason why Jeff Smith is one of the most admired cartoonists working in the medium today.

Steve Morris: As you always do for your own creative process, let's start things with the ending. For the anniversary of *Bone* last year, you published a new story, *Bone: Coda*. What led you to return to the story with a coda that follows on from the finale of your original run?

Jeff Smith: It was the twenty-fifth anniversary and we wanted to do something . . . the question was what. I had loosely sketched up a story that immediately followed the final chapter of *Bone* for a different project that was meant to be a children's book, but ultimately put it on the shelf. During a staff meeting, we hit on the idea of me finishing the new chapter and rounding out the book with behind the scenes essays full of photos and memories, kind of like the extras on a Blu-ray film, but as a companion volume to the *Bone* series. I especially wanted to thank people in the comics community who went out of their way to help me in the early days.

Morris: Going from the original *Bone* comics and returning to that world now, do you feel your approach to how you sequence a page and tell a story has shifted—or was it easy to return back to the style of those first stories?

Smith: I wondered if I could still draw the Bone cousins the way I used to. You're right, styles change and evolve, but the boys came back to me right away, almost as if I never stopped. My line is a little shakier, maybe, and I have a tendency nowadays to work in widescreen panels, but otherwise it felt very much like going home.

Morris: Some of your earliest influences were in animation —and in fact, you started out in animation yourself. When did you decide to make the move into comics? When did you first feel that this was the best medium for telling the story you wanted?

Smith: I always wanted to work in comics. Animation was a way station while I figured out how to break in. Originally the goal was to create a *Bone* comic strip for the newspapers, but I wasn't having much luck.

If I were to narrow it down to one moment, I think the pivot to comic books came during a speech I heard Bill Watterson give at the Festival of Cartoon Art on the Ohio State University campus in 1989. Watterson was lamenting the shrinking size of comic strips since their heyday, and generally warning against the forces of commerce that were stifling creativity. That speech had a profound effect on me, and afterward I went outside and sat under a tree in front of the student union.

I don't know how long I sat there, I lost track of time. What I heard was the death knell of the medium I loved.

At the same time, I had just rediscovered comic books. First [Art] Spiegelman's *Maus*, then [Frank] Miller's *The Dark Knight Returns* lured me into comic book shops only a few years earlier where I discovered underground books like *Love & Rockets*, *Eightball*, and self-published work like *Cerebus*. So that was it. From that moment on, I wanted *Bone* to be a self-published underground comic book. I stood up, returned to the conference and never looked back. No more waiting for someone's permission to draw, and to my surprise, it turned out the space and format of multi-page books suited my skills much better than the four panels of strips.

Morris: How did the setup and creation of Cartoon Books come together, and how important was it for you to have that support structure in place during that time, and moving forward?

Smith: Very important. No one could do this alone. From the very beginning, my wife Vijaya helped me create a business plan and kept the books. Even so, she still had a full time job and I had to write, draw, edit the letters page, create covers and logos . . . by hand . . . before Photoshop, write solicitation texts for the distributors' catalog, and then print the books.

When things took off, and I suddenly was overwhelmed with reorders, shipping, mail, and requests of all kinds, to do appearances or interviews, I had to hire my first assistant, a young comics fan in the [San Francisco] Bay Area named Garrett Chin. But within a few months the workload grew to the point where I asked Vijaya to quit her job and become my partner full-time and run the business end of things. I needed to concentrate on making the comics and promoting them. That worked out pretty well.

Now, twenty-five years later, Vijaya and I have two full-time assistants who help us with traveling to shows, managing our production schedule, and licensing the books and characters. As of now, *Bone* has been translated into thirty languages, with more coming all the time. I still write and draw every line in my comics, but dealing with printers, Hollywood, lawyers, contracts, travel, foreign publishers and all that jazz is dealt with by Vijaya and Kathleen Glosan. Manning the comic convention booth, Photoshop and coloring the books is now done by Tom Gaadt. It's a great group. And we like each other.

Next year will be Kathleen's twentieth year with us, and Tom's eighteenth! Our staff meetings cover business matters as well as creative ones. I count on them every day, and they always have my back.

Morris: For me, what distinguishes *Bone* almost immediately is your sense of character design: the Bone cousins themselves; the dragons; that giant leaf creature . . . What's your process for working out what characters like Fone Bone, Smiley Bone, and Phoney Bone should look like? Their design, their posture, their expression?

Smith: It's really just knowing what you like and trying to get the thing to work the way it needs to. This is definitely an oversimplification, but when I'm drawing, it comes down to two schools of cartooning: Disney —specifically Carl Barks and Walt Kelly, who both came out of that studio with strong senses of character construction and appeal. And *Mad* magazine —the wild and unruly art of Sergio Aragones, Al Jaffee, Don Martin, and Mort Drucker that oozes humor and individuality. And of course, Harvey Kurtzman, the architect of *MAD*. Without Harvey, we'd all be wandering in the wilderness.

Morris: *RASL* was quite a change of pace, perhaps aimed at older readers, and with this strong sci-fi noir influence and a single protagonist. How did you decide on this being your follow-up to *Bone?* Were you deliberately seeking to find something that'd be seen as a marked difference, in terms of tone and content?

Smith: I know, right? What was I thinking? Terry Moore said it freaked him out to see Jeff Smith drawings doing dirty things!

No, it wasn't deliberate. In fact, the concept for *RASL* started out very differently, more cartoony. Early sketches of the main character looked like something out of manga. But the idea evolved as it developed. I started with parallel universes, then layered on *film noir*, and added a dash of Tesla and conspiracy theories . . . the next things I needed were a villain and a femme fatale. It ended up being a smokier, harder comic than *Bone*, not just to be different, but because it was fantastic to work on. I really enjoyed writing and drawing that book.

Morris: From a storytelling perspective, what most strikes me about *RASL* is the choice to use wider panels, feature more "silent" panels, and decompress somewhat. Did you approach this *as* an opportunity to strike outwards, try different modes of storytelling within the comics medium, and experiment with your sequencing?

Smith: I did. The wider panels were a nod to the cinematic origins of *noir*, and the story itself was non-linear to evoke the dislocation that the main character feels living in multiple universes. Writing from a first-person perspective, that is, with the reader only knowing what *RASL* knows or has witnessed personally, was a challenge. It makes exposition really tough. In *Bone*, I could always cut to the bad guys and show them scheming, but in *RASL*, the main character has no idea who the bad guys even are.

As far as my sense of pacing, or style of panel-to-panel transitions go, I didn't consciously change that up at all. I've always done decompressed storytelling. Starting with the first issue of *Bone*, you'll find silent panels and drawn out sequences. That's how I do! Probably because of what I was saying earlier, how I planned and practiced for four-paneled comic strips and then discovered comic books with almost unlimited space —I just stretched out and enjoyed myself.

Morris: People may not have expected you to do a miniseries at DC —but if there was one character that people could ever have predicted you'd work on, I think it would've been Billy Batson. How did you come to the world of work-for-hire, and how did you end up using the Shazam characters?

Smith: It was DC's idea. The way I heard it, during an editorial meeting it was asked if they could get anyone on any project, who and what would it be? The consensus was Kyle Baker on *Plastic Man* and me on *Shazam*. I agreed, because as you said there are elements to the character that suit me. Wizards, mythology and talking tigers. What's not to like?

Morris: What was it like writing someone else's characters —and with DC in general? Did you find there was enough to reach into and work with, to explore?

Smith: Enough. The Rock of Eternity gave me some interesting metaphysics to chew on. Researching the original comics by C. C. Beck and Bill Parker made it clear that Billy and the Captain were two separate individuals that somehow shared the same space. That not only tied into the weird quantum physics of the Rock of Eternity, but also gave me the idea that Captain Marvel was something like a genie in a bottle who could be called upon for help. That notion of jinn mythology helped me explain Tawky Tawny the talking tiger . . . because if I made him a jinn, he could shape shift from man to beast. In the original stories, Tawny was a normal tiger in India that accidentally drank a bowl of magic milk or something.

Anyway, at that point, I had all the characters connected to the powers of the Rock of Eternity through the Wizard. Next, I needed a story and an emotional journey for Billy. I picked the Monster Society of Evil because it is the most famous Captain Marvel adventure from the Golden Age, and also because it's the most awesome title ever. Billy would learn that he had a sister out there somewhere he didn't know about, so he goes from living alone on the street to having family and friends around him. Mary Marvel as the younger sister turned out to be the highlight of the project for me.

I mean, the characters were fun to write and draw, and you can't ask for more than that. Working with DC was great. I had two stipulations before accepting the job. One: that DC would approve my entire script in advance so once I started I could just go without interference. And two: that no other superheroes exist in the world . . . this is a Captain Marvel only world. They agreed, as long as I didn't *say* that no other superheroes exist. Ah! Perfect!

Morris: Your next project was *Tüki: Save the Humans,* a travelling adventure story. It seems like this is a style you're fond of; is it fair to say that you're interested in world-building on the fly; of sending your characters out into an unknown where anything can happen?

Smith: Yes, to an extent. Especially on a longer work, allowing yourself the freedom to explore and follow whims of inspiration keeps the work fresh — not just for me, but for the characters and hopefully the readers. The thing stays alive when the characters are curious and unsure. But you can't make things up out the blue. There need to be rules to the world and structure to the story. An outline.

As you said at the very beginning of this interview, I always start a project by figuring out the ending. This is a serious effort, and it takes time to play with the characters and imagine a journey. It's not hard, and usually the ending comes in an emotional moment of inspiration, but I have to wait for it . . . because until that happens, I don't know if the story is worth telling. Only then do I go back and fill in an outline that will guide the characters and build to that conclusion.

Morris: For *Tüki* you published the story as a webcomic, rather than as a series of single print issues. Was this a response to shifts in the marketplace, and the way people consume comics? Have you had to reconsider the approach that Cartoon Books makes to actually putting out your stories?

Smith: The Internet is changing everything . . . the way we listen to music, how we get our news, how we read, even our politics. Yes, we wanted to dip our toe into the world of webcomics. There are cartoonists over the years whose work online I admire . . . Kate Beaton, Allie Brosh, Faith Erin Hicks, Scott Kurtz, Dash Shaw, to name a few . . . I wanted to take a crack at it. Try an experiment. I figured if it didn't work out, I could always go back to print publishing.

Tuki is an interesting case. I'm about a hundred pages into it, but . . . because on the web you load the story up one or two pages at a time, I approached the project as a series of Sunday comics, like *Flash Gordon* or *Prince Valiant*. That was a lot of fun, but I'm not sure that was the best thing for *Tuki* itself. When we reprinted the story later in comic book form, some of the pages flowed, some didn't. There was a start and stop quality. My bad. Long story short, through no fault of the Internet, my brief, wondrous life as a webcartoonist is over for now. *Tuki* will return, though. It's going to take a little reworking, some major, some minor.

The strip is on hiatus, but it'll be back, just in a different form.

Morris: You've made a habit of being unpredictable and taking on a number of different roles within the comics industry that aren't just writing or drawing comics —right now you're heavily involved in organizing the CXC Festival, for example. With *Tuki* on hiatus and *Bone: Coda* wrapped, what are you currently focused on? Do you have new comics in the works, or are you presently happily occupied elsewhere, with projects like CXC?

Smith: I finally wrapped up the children's book I was working on, and I am currently revamping *Tuki*. It's early days, but it's looking good. My side projects do take up a lot of time. Especially CXC. But these efforts are part of comics to me. They are promotion, not just for my work, but for comics in general, which is something I've always been passionate about. CXC, or Cartoon Crossroads Columbus, combines two things I love: Comics and my hometown. It takes place every Fall. This year will be our third festival, and it seems to be growing fast. It's a four-day festival that focuses on all disciplines of cartooning and cartoonists.

CXC is an outgrowth of the OSU Festival of Cartoon Art that I mentioned earlier where I heard Watterson speak. In fact, Vijaya and I partnered with Lucy Caswell, the founding curator of the Billy Ireland Cartoon Library and the original festival, to launch CXC. My job as president and artistic director is to build a coalition among the art institutions in our city. For example, we might have the Wexner Center for the Arts bringing in animation guests, the OSU Billy Ireland Cartoon Library & Museum and the Columbus College of Art & Design bringing in strip and comic book artists.

Last year, the Wex and the Billy teamed up to bring Garry Trudeau to town. The Columbus Museum of Art sponsored Ron Wimberly, who was the Thurber House Graphic Novelist in Residence and also mounted an exhibition of his work in the museum. The year before that, CMORRISD brought in Art Spiegelman and Françoise Mouly for the show.

We also try to bring together veterans and master cartoonists with the next generation at the comics marketplace downtown in the Columbus Metropolitan Library. Seeing Sergio Aragonés chatting with Katie Skelly, or Jaime Hernandez having dinner with Lalo Alcaraz is kind of what it's about for me. The cartooning community.

I interviewed Raina Telgemeier in front of a full room of young girls who all, when asked, raised their hands to say they want to be cartoonists. I remember how important it was to meet people who had *made it*, who'd been out there. It's a way of paying forward all the generosity that was shown to me when I was starting out. I think that's a big part of all my unpredictable roles, as you called them. Whether it was the Self-Publishing Movement, the Trilogy Tour, editing *Best American Comics*, or even being on the Board of the Comic Book Legal Defense Fund, it's about promoting comics as an art form and supporting the work of other cartoonists.

Also, I get to hang out with all these creative cats. Yes—Comics with a capital "C" keeps me happily occupied, and hopefully will for as long as I can hold a pencil.

"Zapowiada kolejny komiks ze świata, Gnata"!

MARCIN WAINCETEL / 2017

Booklips (November 21, 2017). Published with permission.

Marcin Waincetel: You mentioned once that your earliest forerunner drawings of the Bone cousins—specifically Fone Bone—were created when you were five years old. So, I'm wondering . . . can I say you were a dedicated cartoonist from the age of five? Was that your biggest dream from childhood to tell stories with pictures?

Jeff Smith: Cartoons have always been my favorite thing, no question! The character Bone first appeared when I was five, that's true, so yes, you can say that. I have drawn cartoons my whole life. Unfortunately, I didn't get paid for the first twenty-five years.

Waincetel: Please, correct me if I'm wrong, but I think that *Bone* is—most of all—a wonderful fairy tale. And like Bruno Bettelheim said, fairy tales can help children (but not only them, of course) to solve and understand certain existential problems. They can also sensitize, move us to tears, or make us laugh. Did you want to create a universal story? Because there is something in the *Bone* comic books for everyone—doesn't matter if you're nine or ninety years old!

Smith: I love fairytales. My grandmother would read Grimm's' fairytales to my brother and me when we stayed at her house overnight. She was reading us the uncensored versions, so this was strong stuff! In some ways they are witty, scary, horrible and fascinating because of that; but the true power of those old stories sinks in without you knowing. You experience those imaginary terrors from the safety of your grandmother's lap. It braces your psyche for the future. On a more practical note, comic strips in the newspapers were always designed to appeal to the whole household. Not just to kids, but to the parents that were actually paying for the paper. Many of my heroes, Schulz, Kelly, Foster, Gould, and Barks could be read by all ages.

Waincetel: Is that true that you got mail from your fans in which they ask you to present a great cow race (one of the surrealistic and hilarious scenes from *Bone*)? As far as I know—you didn't plan it! Of course, I ask about this for a reason. You've said that you knew the ending of the *Bone* series from the beginning, but have you ever been susceptible to any suggestions from friends, family or fans, if we're talking about the plot?

Smith: I did know the ending, but my script notes called for Phoney Bone to scam the townspeople in some way to get the Bones in trouble and keep them stuck in the valley as punishment. But I had not come up with what the scam would be. There was a moment when Fone Bone was being prepared to meet Thorn's Gran'ma Ben that I threw in a strange little joke to make the grandmother sound crazy. Thorn mentioned that Gran'ma raced cows—on foot. I thought that was funny in a Monty Python-esque way and gave it no more thought. Once Gran'ma Ben came into the strip, she was a hit and people liked her. Then came the letters! Readers couldn't wait to see Gran'ma Ben in a cow race. How ridiculous and perfect! What could I do? I drew a cow race!

Waincetel: You repeatedly emphasize that you are big fan of Carl Barks (Phoney Bone as a Scrooge McDuck), J. R. R. Tolkien's *Lord of the Rings* (mythological world), Leo Tolstoy's *War and Peace* (epic narrative), Homer's *The Odyssey* (meaning of journey). You are a very talented artist connected to the intertextuality in pop culture. You value the classic stories, right? Many comic enthusiasts believe that *Bone* is also a classic.

Smith: Thank you. I love pop culture. It's a living art. Novels, music, movies, TV, comics. Storytelling. However, one must be able to discern good pop culture from bad. I'm not so much into celebrity worship or gossip, just the art that floats around us at eye and ear level never really intending to be profound, but always telling us the truth.

Waincetel: You started publishing *Bone* in July 1991. That wasn't an obvious time for that kind of comic book. It was a period which is today known as "The Modern Age of Comic Books"—we know it from (for example) the rise of antiheroes in comic books. And it was in this era that you decided to present *Bone*, a strange and brave—at the same time—move!

Smith: I did not have high expectations for *Bone*. I hoped here would be other cartoon-heads out there who would dig my love letter to funny animals and high fantasy. And there were, but I never dreamed it would take off the way it did. A lot of people told me this was a book they either had always wanted to see or a comic they always wanted to make! Luck and timing had something to do with it too. The gritty anti-heroes that were becoming popular could be pretty dark, and many comics publishers at that time were issuing variant covers to boost sales, causing a backlash that sent readers looking for something gentler and less cynical. My little humor comic—published out of our garage by my wife and me—was at the right place at the right time.

Waincetel: Today *Bone* is a bestselling title. But perhaps not everyone knows that it is also an independently published comic book series! It was very risky, I suppose, to create it on your own. But you got support from your family—your wife Vijaya helps you lead your Cartoon Books company. It is proof that, just like in *Bone,* family help and mutual trust is important in real life to realize dreams. Do you agree with this?

Smith: What a wonderful question! Over the thirteen years spent creating *Bone* I often felt like I was on my own journey that paralleled the Bone cousins.' There was luck, travel, opportunity, new friends, and many traps and obstacles around every bend in the river. Somehow, my wife and our two assistants all worked together and managed to steer clear of the rocks!

It is true in every endeavor, on every continent. Trust family and friends . . . and use the strength of your own moral rudder to steer.

Waincetel: Polish readers finally have an opportunity to read the *Bone* series (*Gnat* in the Polish translation). Reviews are more than enthusiastic—and rightly so, it is wonderful. I wonder—are you familiar with any Polish pop culture works or artists? Not necessarily from the comic books medium—I'm asking about literature, art, music, and films, too.

Smith: In my travels I have come across Polish comics. I could not read them, but there are things I very much like about the ones I've seen: the predominance of cartoony artwork, and I've been told there is a distinct independent streak in your comics of the past few decades.

Waincetel: During last year's San Diego Comic Con you announced returning to the world of *Bone* for a new original story featuring Smiley Bone. What can we expect from *Smiley's Dream Book*? And I'm curious—which character from the *Bone* series is your favorite?

Smith: *Smiley's Dream Book* is a picture book for children. Smiley Bone is the most childlike and uninhibited of the cousins, so it was fun to come up with a little adventure using him and a friendly flock of birds. It's mostly visual, but it has a nice ending. My favorite character? It could be any of them depending on the day. But I suppose it has to be Fone Bone. He was the first one I made up, and is the one I most want to be like.

Waincetel: What about the *Bone* feature film? Mark Osborn (*Kung Fu Panda*) is directing, and Adam Kline will write the screenplay. How involved are you in this project? Are you excited about it?
Smith: I am excited about it. I am an executive producer on the film, but ultimately this is Mark's film. We are friends, so we work together, but it's really on his shoulders to bring *Bone* to the screen.

Waincetel: Of course, you are best known as the creator of *Bone*, but you've also created some other titles. *Tuki*, about the first human to leave Africa (two million years ago!), and *RASL*, a hardboiled crime drama about an art thief who jumps to parallel universes to steal valuable treasures. Perhaps you like experimenting with genre?
Smith: I like thinking up crazy stories. When I think of a book I want to write, genre isn't important. I love genre, but what I'm really looking for is tone. I like the way characters behave and react in *noir*, for example, so I put a hardboiled twist and a femme fatale in my science fiction book *RASL*. Of course, *RASL* is really about physics and the possibility that parallel universes might exist. In *Tuki*, my current project about paleontology and evolution, the events take place in an ancient African jungle two million years ago, but the tone I want is like a western, with Tuki playing the part of a gunslinger ranging across the west.

Waincetel: I suspect that you are a fulfilled artist. But perhaps there is something—a challenge, I mean—that you want to take? For example—creating something unusual for your comic book style.
Smith: I feel fortunate that I get to make comics, but I'm never satisfied—it always seems like the newest project is the worst thing I've ever done. It pushes me to fix things, make them better. Each story is a journey to a new destination.

Waincetel: How would you answer the question about the "definition of art?" And by that, I mean your personal way of thinking about art.
Smith: Art is a conversation. It starts from a place we all know and goes exploring. It can be funny, enlightening, disturbing, and even horrifying, but above all it must ring true.

INDEX

ABOUT THE EDITOR

Photo by Breanne Lejeune, The Ohio State University

Frederick Luis Aldama is Distinguished University Professor at The Ohio State University. He is the award-winning author, coauthor, and editor of forty books, including *Latinx Superheroes in Mainstream Comics*; *The Cinema of Robert Rodriguez*; *Latinx Comic Book Storytelling: An Odyssey by Interview*; *Long Stories Cut Short: Fictions from the Borderlands*; and *Tales from la Vida: A Latinx Comics Anthology*.

CPSIA information can be obtained
at www.ICGtesting.com
Printed in the USA
BVHW051458270919

559608BV00002B/2/P